THE SIGNET BOOK OF CHOCOLATE

In this book you will find the fascinating history of chocolate; the process of producing chocolate; the myths and mystique of chocolate; the full nutritional data about chocolate; and all the ways that chocolate may be enjoyed, with tempting recipes and invaluable tips about storing and serving. As an especially practical feature, there is a mouth-watering, brand-by-brand rating of chocolates from all over the world, including both familiar candy bars and the most costly and exotic confections on earth.

Nibble on the first page of this superlative guide, and you won't stop until you've devoured every word.

"A fine book that could turn out to be a classic."

—PUBLISHERS WEEKLY

THE SIGNET BOOK OF CHOCOLATE

The Signet Book of Chocolate

Carol Ann Rinzler

A SIGNET BOOK
NEW AMERICAN LIBRARY
TIMES MIRROR

NAL BOOKS ARE ALSO AVAILABLE AT DISCOUNTS IN BULK QUANTITY FOR INDUSTRIAL OR SALES-PROMOTIONAL USE. FOR DETAILS, WRITE TO PREMIUM MARKETING DIVISION, NEW AMERICAN LIBRARY, INC., 1301 AVENUE OF THE AMERICAS, NEW YORK, NEW YORK 10019.

Library of Congress Catalog Card Number: 77-76650

A hardcover edition was published by St. Martin's Press Incorporated

SIGNET TRADEMARK REG. U.S. PAT. OFF. AND FOREIGN COUNTRIES
REGISTERED TRADEMARK—MARCA REGISTRADA
HECHO EN CHICAGO, U.S.A.

SIGNET, SIGNET CLASSICS, MENTOR, PLUME AND MERIDIAN BOOKS *are published by The New American Library, Inc. 1301 Avenue of the Americas, New York, New York 10019*

FIRST SIGNET PRINTING, DECEMBER, 1978

1 2 3 4 5 6 7 8 9

PRINTED IN THE UNITED STATES OF AMERICA

For my mother and father

Acknowledgments

For the professional and technical information without which this manuscript would have been incomplete, I am deeply grateful to a number of people who were especially generous with their time and their knowledge, either in personal interviews or in detailed correspondence.

Hy Becker and Al Bianchi of Cella's Confections, Joseph Blumenthal of W-J International, and Edmond Opler of World's Finest Chocolate offered fascinating glimpses into the history and development of the chocolate industry.

And the following people provided much needed information and anecdotes about the industry, the individual chocolate manufacturers, and their products: James Atkinson, Kenneth Bowers, Trecie Fennell, Estavan Giannoni, Mme Henriette Girardi-Corné, L. E. Godfrey, Joseph F. Grimes, Richard K. Gully, Max Hess, Steven Korsen, Eli Meshulam, Shelley Miller, J. H. Moore, Ruth Morrison, Henry Nimmon, James Nixon, Thomas North, Richard T. O'Connor, Page Poore, Gil Rabin, Walter Scheurzinger, B. H. Siebers, Denton Thorne, Richard Van Doren, Lincoln Warrell, Judith A. Wilson, and Richard Wilson. Dorothy Hunerfauth, Marsha Lane, Loys Malmgren and Annette Pearlman helped me locate precisely the recipes I needed.

Having thanked them all, let me add that any errors or omissions in the manuscript are mine alone, as are all the stated preferences and product evaluations.

June 1976 CAROL ANN RINZLER

Contents

PART ONE: FROM THE COCOA BEAN TO THE CHOCOLATE BAR

PART TWO: A CONSUMER'S GUIDE TO CHOCOLATE

THE SIGNET BOOK OF CHOCOLATE

PART ONE

FROM THE COCOA BEAN TO THE CHOCOLATE BAR

1: THE HISTORY OF CHOCOLATE

Like wine, chocolate has mythological roots that are mixed with religion. Like fine cheese, it is a food whose taste and texture depend upon its fat content, its seasoning, and occasionally, its having been aged. Like coffee, it is usually a blend of roasted beans, and like tea, it was once the object of a fierce international trade rivalry.

Unlike the others, though, chocolate is rarely taken seriously, being regarded instead as a dieter's indulgence or a child's treat.

But chocolate is indeed fascinating. Well made and sensibly enjoyed, it is a food for the most philosophical gourmet, and its history is, in the best sense of the word, a romance.

Chocolate Before the Sixteenth Century

Most of what we know about the history of chocolate before 1519, when the Spanish explorer Hernando Cortez first tasted it at the court of the Aztec emperor Montezuma, is based upon conjecture, myth, and circumstantial evidence.

Botanists tell us that the first cocoa trees probably grew wild in the Amazon or Orinoco valleys more than four thousand years ago. Archaeologists surmise that cocoa was cultivated for the first time by the Mayans, who took it with them when they migrated to the Yucatán about the seventh century A.D. The Aztecs, too, appear to have carried cocoa seeds with them wherever they wandered, up and down Central America.

The derivation of the word "chocolate" is certainly Aztec/Mayan. It comes from *chocolatl*, which is what the Indians called the cold bitter drink they made by mixing ground cocoa beans with liquid. The precise origins of *chocolatl*, however, are in doubt. One possibility is that the word is a combination of two Mayan words, *choco* (warm) and *latl* (beverage), but since *chocolatl* was usually served cold, this seems unlikely. A second possibility is that *latl* actually means water, and that *choco* describes the sound made when the ground beans were mixed with the liquid, whirled in an earthenware or golden cup with a wooden implement called a molinet. The molinet, which looked something like a child's wooden hammer, made the drink frothy, which raises a third possibility, that *choco* meant froth, or foam. (The word "cocoa" is easier to trace. It appears to have come directly from the Aztec/Mexican word *cachuatl*, which comes from *cacahuazintl*, meaning the fruit or pod of the cocoa tree.) Legend says *chocolatl* was an intoxicating drink; science says maybe.

Like coffee beans and tea leaves, cocoa beans contain stimulants: caffeine (which is found in a number of plants) and theobromine (which is found only in cocoa and chocolate). The early cocoa beans were almost certainly more potent than the carefully cultivated ones we use today, which have been bred especially for their mild, pleasant flavors and precisely regulated temperaments. Then, too, the Indians' *chocolatl* was often made by mixing the ground beans with fermented corn mash or with wine, instead of water, and the quantities in which the drink was consumed would have multiplied any intoxicating effects. At Montezuma's court, for example, more than two thousand cups of *chocolatl* were poured every day. The emperor himself drank fifty of them and may well have believed that every single cup was blessed by the Aztec god Quetzalcoatl.

In almost every culture with multiple gods, there is usually the legend of the one special god who, having given a divine possession or prerogative to mankind, is punished for the deed. Among the Olympians, it was Prometheus, who stole fire from heaven and was condemned to eternal torture for his crime. Among the Aztec gods, it was Quetzalcoatl. The

Indians believed that he brought the seeds of the cocoa tree from the Garden of Life and gave them to man. For a while afterward, Quetzalcoatl continued to live in harmony with gods and man, but eventually he fell from grace and was banished. Before he left, he promised that he would return; most historians agree that the hospitality with which Cortez was greeted by the Aztecs resulted from his being mistaken for the returning god.

The myth might vary from area to area, but unquestionably the Indians considered cocoa a special crop. In Mexico, at the start of every planting season, the Itza Indians are said to have sacrificed a prisoner to Tonacatecutli, the goddess of food, and Calchiutlucue, the goddess of water. Prisoners were given cups of *chocolatl* in the belief that it would turn their hearts to chocolate. Then the heart was torn from the body and offered to the goddesses. In Nicaragua the gods (or the populace) appear to have been less bloodthirsty. There, cocoa farmers attempted to placate Quetzalcoatl (whom they called the god of the moon) and ensure the fertility of the crop by abstaining from sexual activity for at least two weeks before sowing the seeds.

Usually the ceremonies worked, which is to say that the cocoa tree, a prolific bloomer in congenial climates, almost always produced a more than adequate crop of beans. And so it went, season after season, for several thousand years.

None of this, however, seemed to impress the Spanish conquistadors about to make their way into Mexico. The fact that cocoa beans were used as money, did.

The Spanish Monopoly, 1502-1606

The modern age of chocolate begins with one of those questions that nag at historians but don't really affect the flow of historical events. Where was Christopher Columbus in 1502, when he became the first European to see and taste chocolate? *

According to some accounts, he was in Nicaragua, landing there at the end of July. According to others, he was off the coast of Mexico, and the chocolate was brought to his ship by Indians who rode out in canoes to greet him. However, Columbus left it wherever he found it, too taken with his search for new routes to the East and its spices to see the potential in the cocoa beans.

Seventeen years later, it was quite a different story. Arriving at the Aztec court in Veracruz, Cortez was unimpressed with the taste of *chocolatl,* but fascinated by the golden cups in which the drink was served and with the use of cocoa beans as money. Reports say that ten beans would buy a rabbit; one hundred beans would buy a slave.† And the tribute from Montezuma's defeated enemies included chests of cocoa beans and ground chocolate, along with the more conventional booty.

Not for nothing was Cortez a son of Spain: With the same canny instinct that had sent the Spaniards out over the world to begin with, he did his patriotic duty, immediately establishing a cocoa plantation under the Spanish flag, to grow "money" for the king. Leaving Mexico, he did something even more important in the long run. He took beans with him, and as he traveled, he planted them: on Trinidad; on Haiti; on Fernando Po, the island off Africa from which, three hundred years later, a single cocoa tree would be imported to form the base of the gigantic modern cocoa industry on Africa's west coast. Wherever the tree would grow, the Spanish planted it. As a result, a century later, even when Spain's monopoly on chocolate had ended, its domination of the trade remained secure. Until the eighteenth century

* Until the nineteenth century, when eating chocolate was invented and a distinction drawn between cocoa or hot chocolate (a liquid) and chocolate (a solid food), all chocolate meant drinking chocolate, some variation or other on the basic drink, *chocolatl.*

† Where there is money, there are counterfeiters. Among the Indians, they hollowed out the cocoa bean shells and filled them with dirt, reserving the valuable beans for themselves.

almost all the chocolate used in Europe passed, at one point or another, through Spanish hands.

Crossing the Borders, 1606-1780

At home the Spanish were circumspect. They drank chocolate ground by monks in monasteries, and they drank it practically in secret. While the English and Dutch navies continued to dump "worthless" bags of cocoa beans off captured Spanish ships, the Spanish hoarded their supplies.

But no secret stays a secret forever. In 1606 an Italian gentleman named Antonio Carletti is said to have been the first person to carry chocolate from Spain into Italy. From there, it made its way to the Austrian court, and after that, the progress of chocolate through Europe was mostly a matter of royal marriages.

Anne of Austria married Louis XIII of France and took her chocolate with her. Spain's Maria Theresa, a passionate devotee, took her chocolate to France, too, when she was betrothed to Louis XIV. Almost immediately a royal chocolate-maker was appointed and the drink became quite the rage as well as a subject for consideration by doctors and the clergy.

In Mexico chocolate had already been the subject of a theological donnybrook. In the late 1600s the ladies of the land were accustomed to having their chocolate served to them in church. They said it prevented fainting and "weakness." When one bishop forbade the practice, the ladies took themselves and their entourages to another church, and the offending clergyman, it was rumored, later died of a cup of poisoned chocolate. It was a fearful *scandale*.

On a higher level, the Bishop of Rome declared, in 1662 *Liquidum non frangit jejunum.* [Liquids (including chocolate) do not break the fast.] It is likely that this decision was based on the fact that chocolate, like so many herbs, spices, plants, and special foods, was thought of as a medicine, as a panacea for most, if not all, human ills. Certainly at this point it was usually prepared by apothecaries, who were familiar with the grinding mortar and pestle, rather than by confectioners. Thomas Gage, in *A New Survey of the West Indies* (1648), explained that drinking five cups of chocolate every day for twelve years had turned him into a tower of good health, a view that was favored by most contemporary consumers. If one considers how few truly effective medications were available at the time, it is hard to blame them. Many Europeans thought of chocolate as an aphrodisiac. Madame Du Barry is said to have given it to her men, and Casanova said he used it instead of champagne as an inducement to romance. They may have been on the right track, but for the wrong reasons. Caffeine and theobromine, the stimulants in chocolate, can produce an irritating, diuretic effect. Moreover, it was common at the time to add quantities of pepper to chocolate, and pepper, too, can scratch tender membranes, which is what the supposed aphrodisiac, cantharis, does. Whatever the case, no one has ever shown that chocolate significantly raised the population of western Europe.

By the end of the century a number of quibblers began to question the safety of some of the additives commonly found in cocoa and chocolate. The various European countries had never been benevolent in their relationships with one another, and the chocolate trade was no exception. Adulterated chocolate—containing starches, shells, and sometimes brick dust (which gave it a nifty red-brown color)—was often sold, at a huge profit, as the real thing.

Such practices never slowed, even for a moment, the surging growth of the cocoa market.

To get an idea of how sales were soaring, it is only necessary to learn that by 1763 the British beer and ale interests already felt threatened enough to call for legislation restricting the manufacture of chocolate. In 1704 Frederick I of Prussia took a more pragmatic view. Impressed by the growing imports of chocolate, he simply imposed a tax of two *thalers* on every purchase.

In the meantime, though Spain still controlled the cultivation of chocolate, other countries were moving in bit by bit. The French, for example, planted cocoa on Martinique about

1660 and took it to Bahia (Brazil) around 1750. The English, who had once concentrated on more northerly explorations, began to move into the West Indies. Factories for processing the cocoa beans, which were still produced mainly in Spanish-held areas, were springing up all over Europe. There was Fry & Sons in England (1728), von de Lippe in Germany (1765), and there was one factory on the banks of the Neponset River in Massachusetts that by 1780 had become the Walter Baker Company, the oldest chocolate manufacturer in the United States.

Chocolate was made by hand, ground with mortar and pestle or between hand-driven stone grinding discs. In 1765, that changed. James Watt had perfected his steam engine, and within a few years it was used to run the chocolate mills. In 1780 the first machine-ground chocolate is reported to have been produced in a factory near Barcelona.

New Techniques and Changing Tastes, 1780-1900

During the nineteenth century, there were two distinct revolutions within the chocolate industry.

The first was the Industrial Revolution, the same majestic sweep of mechanization that altered manufacturing processes throughout the civilized world. The second was more subtle, a product revolution that grew quite naturally from the machines.

The new mechanical marvels were steam-driven grinders, chocolate presses, roasters, machines to clean the beans and sweep away the shells and other debris, refiners to smooth the chocolate, mixing machines to combine it with other ingredients. There is a fully detailed description of how each machine works and its role in chocolate-manufacturing in Chapter 2.

The creation of solid chocolate. Whether ground by hand in the old mortar and pestle or by the new steam driven mills, chocolate was still chocolate liquor, the liquidy paste extracted from cocoa beans and hardened into cakes used to make a drink that hadn't really changed since Cortez first tasted it in Veracruz. In 1828, however, a Dutch chemist named Coenraad van Houten filed a patent for "chocolate powder." In doing so, he lay the groundwork for a whole new kind of chocolate.

Van Houten had made his powder by pouring chocolate liquor into a screw-type press,* and then turning the screw so that the press plate came down hard on the chocolate liquor, squeezing out most of the cocoa butter. Cocoa beans (and, of course, chocolate liquor) contain about 53-percent cocoa butter, so van Houten was left with a brown, flaky powder. Although it was higher in fat content than most of the cocoas we buy today, it was essentially the same product, made in essentially the same way.

The next question was, what to do with the extra cocoa butter.

When solidified pure chocolate liquor is too hard and bitter for pleasant eating, adding extra cocoa butter makes it more palatable. It took about twenty years for an English chocolate company to do just that. In 1847 Fry and Sons introduced "eating chocolate," a combination of chocolate liquor, extra cocoa butter, and sugar. About thirty years after that, about 1880, a Swiss manufacturer named Rodolphe Lindt came up with the precise combination of ingredients for a chocolate that would, literally, melt in your mouth. By then, of course, his compatriots Daniel Peter and Henri Nestlé had already created milk chocolate by mixing condensed milk with chocolate liquor and sugar (Vevey, Switzerland, 1876).†

Solid, or "eating," chocolate was clearly the product of the future.

Making chocolate smoother. So long as chocolate liquor was used only to make liquid chocolate, no one cared whether or not it had lumps and gritty particles, since these

*According to some sources, Diderot's *Encyclopedia* is reputed to show a similar machine in the background of an illustration of a chocolate shop, but since van Houten was the first to file a patent, he is usually credited with the invention.

† Milk was first mixed in liquid chocolate, as a drink, about 1730.

disappeared when the chocolate was mixed with water, wine, or milk. An acceptable solid chocolate, however, had to be smooth and possibly silky on the tongue.

The Mexicans had smoothed their chocolate somewhat by rubbing it with stone rollers in stone troughs. The nineteenth-century Europeans, specifically the Swiss, adapted the principle and invented refiners that smoothed the chocolate liquor by passing it between porcelain discs or by rubbing it against itself in a procedure called *conching* (see page [25]). As a result, they were soon able to produce a distinctively smooth chocolate with a particularly mellow flavor. Today, that kind of chocolate is still used as the benchmark against which all others can be measured.

The Twentieth Century

All the basic forms of chocolate had been developed by the end of the nineteenth century, but during the past seventy years we have seen the creation of such specialties as:

Filled chocolates (molded shells for candies or bars into which a filling is poured, rather than firm centers, which are dipped into a chocolate coating), produced for the first time in 1913 by Swiss *chocolatier* Jules Sechaud.

Candy bars, including the most popular chocolate-coated ones, which were first produced about 1911, but reached their noblest heights during World War II when Hershey developed a six-hundred-calorie, survival-diet chocolate bar for the Armed Forces.

Compound chocolate, which is made by adding vegetable fats rather than cocoa butter to chocolate liquor. Compound chocolate melts at lower temperatures than ordinary chocolate (cocoa butter, unlike most other vegetable fats, will remain solid at room temperature), and is, therefore, eminently suited for coatings on ice cream.

Used that way, it doesn't taste discernibly different than ordinary chocolate, although you can taste the difference between two solid bars of the different candies.

Artificial chocolate, a flavoring made of chemical ingredients without any cocoa beans or chocolate at all. For manufacturers such as bakers and makers of chocolate drinks, this flavoring has the advantage of being free from the price fluctuations of real cocoa. As a minor ingredient in cakes or cookies, it is probably indistinguishable from the real thing; it is more obvious in chocolate drinks.

In addition to these product innovations, there have been technological improvements in the past sixty or seventy years, as the basic machinery of the nineteenth century was refined and modified. But the most significant changes in the chocolate industry of late have come in marketing, in the consolidation of the major companies, and in the changes in the basic source of cocoa.

The changing of the guard. Until the turn of the twentieth century, almost all cocoa beans were grown in the Americas and the West Indies; in 1810, fully 50 percent of all the cocoa beans in the world were grown in just one country, Venezuela.

By the late 1890s, however, the fledgling industry in West Africa, along the "golden" coast, had been born. By 1935 it had grown so enormously that Africa—specifically the areas we now call Ghana, the Ivory Coast, and Nigeria—was producing more than twice as many cocoa beans as the Americas. By 1970 they were producing three times as much. Today, the ratio is again slightly more than two to one in favor of the African countries. The Asian countries also scored impressive gains, although, in absolute terms, far lower than the African. The production in the Philippines, for example, rose from five long tons per year to forty-three plus.

The following chart gives a quick and impressive idea of how the control of cultivation has shifted.

Cocoa Bean Production in long tons—2,240 lbs.

	1900	1935	1970	1976
Africa (Cameroun, Ghana, Ivory Coast, Nigeria, *et al.*)	20	483	950+	990+
The Americas (Brazil, Ecuador, Venezuela, *et al.*)	59	186	300	431+
West Indies Dominican Republic, Trinidad, *et al.*)	31	51	45+	59+
Asia (New Guinea, Philippines, *et al.*)	5	7	43+	40+

NOTE: These figures are adapted from "Cocoa Statistics," Gill and Duffus, Inc. (London, England, 1970) and from a 1976 Gill and Duffus report.

There is one important *caveat* that must be added to these figures. Together, three African countries—Ghana, 395+ long tons; Nigeria, 215+ long tons; and the Ivory Coast, 165+ long tons—account for 57 percent of the world's cocoa beans. Brazil, with its yearly production of 171+ long tons, brings the total up to about 70 percent. But what these countries are producing are the *base beans* used in almost every cocoa and chocolate. The *flavor beans,* used to create special nuances in chocolate bars are grown in smaller batches. Costa Rica, for example, which produces one of the world's great flavor beans, has an annual crop of something like seven long tons.

The change in manufacturing. For the better part of four hundred years, making chocolate, and later cocoa and chocolate, was pretty much a straight-line affair. The beans were brought in from one of the cultivating countries and converted to a finished product by one man or one manufacturer.

Today the first steps in chocolate-making—grinding the beans to make chocolate liquor, pressing the chocolate liquor to make cocoa, and adding cocoa butter to the chocolate liquor to make chocolate—are an industry in themselves, with major manufacturing firms selling each of these products (chocolate liquor, cocoa, and chocolate) to various food-producing companies.

A single company, such as the massive De Zaan of Holland (a subsidiary of W. R. Grace), may control as much as 2 percent of the world's market. In the United States there are a number of venerable firms, including Guittard, a west coast company that is the oldest privately owned chocolate-maker in America, that deal solely in sales to manufacturers of consumer products. They are called industrial chocolate companies.

The consolidation of the chocolate companies. As a result of these changes, the chocolate industry, like almost every other, has dwindled from a fine collection of independent manufacturers to a relative handful of companies.

At one time there were more than sixty independent, American-owned companies selling consumer goods (finished chocolate candy) in the United States. Today a significant number of the thirty-odd companies whose chocolate bars and boxed chocolate assortments appear in retail stores here are foreign exporters who make their product abroad. Nearly 52 percent of these companies are subsidiaries of large American or foreign corporations. This include such grand old names as Stuckey's and Whitman (Pet Foods), Pangburn (Riviana), and among the foreign companies, Germany's Sprengel (now part of Nabisco), Switzerland's Suchard and Tobler (Interfood), Holland's Van Houten (part of The Monheim Group, Germany's largest chocolate manufacturer), Ireland's Williams & Woods, and Germany's Sarotti (Nestlé).

This kind of consolidation may not always affect quality—Godiva, the Belgian chocolates, are still as luxurious today, when they are made by a division of Campbell Foods, as they were when they were made abroad—but it certainly affects variety. Perhaps the entry of the Communist Chinese (who now sell boxed chocolates in the United States) and the Russians (who may, although they haven't as yet) will add some new spice to the market.

Which brings us to the last essential question: Who eats the world's chocolate?

Between them, the United States and Europe consume about 70 percent of every year's cocoa crop. Per capita, the Swiss outeat everyone else, gobbling down 22 pounds of chocolate every year, for every man, woman, and child in the country. The English are next; they consume about 15.4 pounds of chocolate per capita each year. The Germans follow (13.8 pounds per capita), then the Belgians (13.6), and the Swedes and the Austrians (11.6 each). The Americans are far behind. Per-capita consumption of chocolate in the United States averages out to about a mere 10 pounds per capita each year.

2: HOW CHOCOLATE IS MADE

The Central American Indians called the cocoa tree a gift of the gods, and the great Swedish naturalist Linnaeus formally named it *Theobroma cacao,* "the food of the gods."

Today, Quetzalcoatl's legendary gift still grows wild in parts of South America, but with the exception of a few flowering exhibition trees, such as the one at the Brooklyn Botanic Gardens in New York and those at Hershey's Chocolate World in Pennsylvania, it has never been successfully cultivated more than 20 degrees north or south of the equator. It grows best, in fact, within 10 degrees of the equator, in Latin America, the Caribbean, Africa, and parts of Asia.

The tree is an evergreen, with brilliant leaves that start out pale green, pink, or red, and change to a glossy dark green as they mature. It produces flowers and fruit all year long; there is hardly a day in the year when cocoa is not being harvested somewhere in the world.

The fruit of the cocoa tree is a pod with seeds in it. The pods grow right out of the trunk, as well as along the branches, and with careful tending in trees grown from seed, pods will begin to appear about the fifth year of growth. The pods, shaped like long melons, turn golden or red as they grow, depending on what kind of beans they hold inside.

According to botanists, there are two basic types of beans, the Criollos and the Forasteros.

Forasteros are found in hardy, thick-walled pods, which can be grown more easily and in greater abundance than the thinner-skinned and delicate Criollos. The African Accra, a mild bean, and the Brazilian Bahia, darker and stronger-flavored, are both Forasteros. Between them, these two beans make up most of the world's cocoa crop. Because there are so many of them and because their flavors are relatively neutral, the Accras and Bahias are base beans, upon which most of the world's chocolate is built.

The Criollos, on the other hand, are the flavor beans. Criollos such as the Maracaibo, Caracas, Java, and Samoa (cocoa beans are named for the places in which they are grown) are used to create aromatic, nutty, or floral nuances in the basic chocolate blend.

It is rare to find a plantation where only one of these beans is grown. In fact, the hybridization of cocoa beans has been so thorough that beans of the Criollo and Forastero types may even show up on the same tree. Botanists mostly agree, therefore, that all beans fall within one of these two primary types. A number of chocolate people, though, argue that there is a third major strain. Just exactly what it is, is open to discussion.

Some people plump for the Trinitario, a cross between Criollo and Forastero that sprang up on the island of Trinidad. Others say that the Nacional fills the bill, specifically a Nacional called Arriba, which grows only in Ecuador. The Arriba has a distinctive aromatic taste that disappears completely if the bean is grown anywhere other than in its native country. Botanists, unmoved by such chauvinism, insist that the Nacional is still just a Forastero at heart.

Wine fanciers have always made a ritual out of tasting a wine and then reeling off the name of the grape from which it was made, along with the place and time of its birth. Coffee connoisseurs, too, can often tell you what beans are in their favorite blends. With chocolate bars, though, that impressive kind of parlor trick just won't work. Distinctive though the flavors, colors, and aromas of the various cocoa beans may be, it is virtually impossible for anyone to identify them once they have gone into a finished batch of chocolate.

There is one exception. If you were to buy a chocolate bar made and sold locally in one of the major cocoa-producing countries—say, Ghana or Brazil—the odds are that it would have been made from cheap, plentiful native beans. So the taste you get will probably be pure Accra or pure Bahia. All other chocolates are blends of many kinds of beans.

An expert can easily identify a single bean if he cracks and tastes it straight out of the roaster. He may even be able to tell you what bean went into an unblended chocolate liquor, the paste produced from the first grinding of the cocoa beans. But the same expert can talk only in generalities about a blended chocolate, liquor, or bar. He can say that it is "mild," or "floral," or "nutty," but he can only guess—an informed guess, to be sure—as to what exact beans went into the blend.

The point is that there is an infinite number of possible combinations from which any chocolate manufacturer can produce "his" special taste. (That's why the major companies can maintain their characteristic flavors year after year, regardless of the inevitable crop failures.) How they actually make and blend the chocolate is a complex process that starts, naturally enough, with the harvest of the beans.

From Harvest to Factory

Most cocoa plantations run two harvest seasons, a main season and a midcrop harvest. Both last for several months at a time, so that the plantations are nearly always in full operation.

The harvest begins with the pods being cut down from the tree. Once down, they are split open. Inside, the cocoa beans lie embedded in a white pulpy mass. Since it is impossible at this point to separate the beans from the clinging mass, both are scooped out of the husk. In the air the beans change from cream-colored to lavender and purple as they oxidize.

Freshly harvested beans are bitter and acid to the taste. Before they can be sent off to the cocoa and chocolate manufacturers, this acid taste must be toned down, and the clinging white pulp must be removed. Fermentation does both.

In the most primitive processing the pulp and beans are piled into a hole in the ground and covered with leaves. They may, in more advanced processing, be piled on top of the ground and covered, or, in modern fashion, they may be heaped into wooden boxes with lids. In any case, the result is the same: as they lie there, the temperature in the mass rises—sometimes over 110°F.—and fermentation begins. Strictly speaking, it is the white pulp that ferments. Its sugars are converted to alcohol and carbon dioxide; then bacterial action turns the alcohol into acetic acid, the same substance that gives vinegar (and spoiled wine) its distinctive taste. This chemical chain of events visibly affects the cocoa beans, turning them a familiar brown. It also kills off their germ, so that they cannot sprout; separates them from the white pulp, which will be discarded; hardens the beans' coverings into shells; and softens the acid taste by allowing the development of essential oils that will later flower into the characteristic lush chocolate taste and aroma.

It usually takes one to three days for this process to work on Criollo beans; Forasteros ordinarily require about a week.

Fermented beans must be dried before they are shipped so that they will not rot in transit. Sometimes this is accomplished the old-fashioned way, by spreading them out to dry in the sun. But if the climate in which they have grown is too moist, or if the weather is too uncertain, or if the grower simply wants to be sure that he can control the process, they will be dried by hot-air blowers as they lie in long bins inside wooden huts, safely away from the elements.

From Beans to Chocolate

After drying, the brown cocoa beans, which have lost almost all of their moisture and about half their weight, are packed into burlap sacks and sent on their various ways around the world.

Arrival at the factory. Since cocoa beans come from tropical areas where insect infestation is commonplace if not inevitable, the first thing that is likely to happen to them when they arrive at the plant is fumigation. Still in their burlap sacks, the beans will be piled in an airtight room and fumigating gases—usually methyl bromiae—are pumped in. After a time long enough to ensure the demise of any live bugs and any eggs that may have been laid while the beans were traveling, the air in the room is mechanically cleansed and the beans are taken out to be stored.

They may be stored right in their sacks, in cool, airy rooms, dry enough to prevent the growth of molds and other kinds of deterioration. Or the sacks may be opened and the beans poured into storage silos where the same cool, dry conditions prevail.

When it is time for the cocoa beans to be used, they will be taken from the sacks or silos and sent through an elaborate cleaning machine: in essence, a series of sieves that separate the beans from rocks, pebbles, dust, and other miscellaneous debris that is blown away by air currents. Then the beans are sorted into batches, according to size so that all can be fully roasted. If all the beans were roasted together, the large ones might end up raw and the little ones overdone.

Sorted, the beans proceed to the roaster.

Roasting. The lovely taste and smell of chocolate begin to develop during fermentation, when essential oils are released within the cocoa beans. Like coffee and nuts, however, cocoa beans need roasting to bring out the best in them.

There are three general degrees of roast: a low, or "raw," one, which heats the beans just enough to make it easy to get the shells off*; a medium roast; and a high, or "full,"

* Some processors shell the beans before roasting by blanching them.

roast. Both time and temperature can be juggled to produce any of these. A long time in the roaster can leave the beans "raw" if the temperature is low enough; a short time in a very hot roaster can produce fully roasted beans.

It shouldn't come as a surprise to hear that different kinds of beans take different kinds of roasts to bring out their best flavor and aroma. Criollos, for example, ordinarily take a lower roast, while Forasteros taste best when fully roasted. There are variations, too, within each group, and there are variations in national tastes that can determine how throughly beans are to be roasted. In Spain beans are traditionally given a high roast, as are beans meant for dark chocolate made in Germany. In Switzerland and the United States, on the other hand, a generally lower roast is the rule. Finally, how the beans will be used can also affect how they will be roasted. Cocoa powder, for example, has a stronger aroma than chocolate, so a hypothetical batch of beans would probably be roasted more fully if it were going to be used for cocoa than if it were going to be used for chocolate.

Cocoa-bean roasters look a lot like those used for coffee and nuts. There are two general types: a rotating-drum roaster, which is heated by gas or flame, and a continuous-flow roaster, in which beans are heated by air currents as they travel along on a moving belt. Although they may be huge, rotating drums can also be small "batch" roasters, used to roast a small group of special beans under easily controlled conditions. The continuous-flow roasters, however, are usually, by their general nature, large factory machines used for large batches of beans.

Whichever type of roaster is used, the end result is the same: a fragrant, warm bean whose shell is dry and easily cracked.

If you were following the bean through the chocolate-making process, this is the first moment at which you would begin to get a hint of the product to come. Until now, all talk about flavor and aroma has been promises, but when you crack open a roasted bean, you find the nibs, small, dark brown particles that are the basis of all cocoa and chocolate.*

Cracking and winnowing. Before you can taste them, the nibs have to be separated from the shells. Cracking a few at a time by hand is fun, but hardly practical in large batches, so the next step is the cracking and winnowing machine. Here the beans are broken open by heavy, toothed arms, designed to keep the nibs in large, unbroken pieces. The nibs and the shells together then fall into the winnower, a series of sieves that resemble those in the cleaning machines. Again, the shells and debris are blown away, so that at the end only the clean nibs remain.

However, like the proverbial pig used up right to his squeal, the cocoa beans are fully utilized. The shells are ground for fertilizer, cattle feed, and as a source of theobromine, which is used in medicines and some foods.

Grinding the beans. But the nibs are the stars of the show. Roasted, shelled, and clean, they smell and taste like chocolate, however bitter. Now they will be used to produce something that looks like chocolate, too.

Cocoa-bean nibs are high in fat. When they are ground between heavy stone or steel discs (grinding mills), they are heated, and the cocoa butter is liquefied and released. The result is a thick, dark paste called chocolate liquor.†

In some plants an extra dollop or two of cocoa butter may be added to the chocolate liquor to make it softer and more pliable, but the mass can simply be hardened in bar molds and sold just as it is, as baking chocolate, the hard, bitter bar or square that is the most basic form of edible chocolate you can buy in the United States.

It is far more likely, though, that the liquor will be used to make either cocoa powder or chocolate. Since these two

* As a matter of fact, plain roasted beans can be cracked open and eaten like, say, pistachio nuts; they are sold that way, as snack food, in Mexico.

† Chocolate liquor may be made from one kind of bean or it may be made from a blend of nibs. In fact, many manufacturers say that right before grinding is an ideal time to create a specific blend. Ordinarily, the liquor is a paste, but at temperatures above 88°F. it will liquefy.

are made in completely different ways, it seems logical to look at them separately.

Cocoa powder. To make cocoa powder, the manufacturer pours chocolate liquor into a press and simply presses most of the cocoa butter out of it, leaving a dry, solid cake. When this cake is pulverized, the result is cocoa powder, which can be packed into tins just as it is (like Hershey's plain cocoa) or can be mixed with other ingredients.

The most common is vanilla or vanillin, and for all practical purposes, cocoa with either of these flavorings can be considered almost plain cocoa. But you can also find a variety of other things in instant, or quick, cocoa—sugar, starches, milk powders, and a fistful of vitamins and minerals. (If you find these on the label, the odds are that you will also find a preservative listed; cocoa is remarkably stable, but the extra ingredients may not be.)

Cocoa powder may also be Dutched. This means that it has been treated with an alkali, commonly 3-percent anhydrous potassium carbonate, in the bean stage, as nibs, or even as chocolate liquor. The result is a darker, mellower cocoa. Whether that also means "better" is a matter of personal taste.

Chocolate. Cocoa powder is chocolate liquor with most of the cocoa butter taken out. In common usage, chocolate (other than bitter, baking chocolate) is chocolate liquor with extra cocoa butter added.

Cocoa butter is an unusual fat. Unlike most vegetable fats, it stays solid at room temperature, melting only at 92 or 93°F., the normal temperature of the human tongue. It resists oxidation and rancidity with a vengeance, and under normal cool, dry storage conditions it will stay fresh for years, which is why plain dark chocolate stores so well. It is rarely as thoroughly refined as other fats, and like many other foods can cause allergic reactions. But it is still widely and effectively used in a lot of different cosmetics, including skin oils, suntan lotions, soaps, and creams.

The most important use to which it is put when it is extracted from chocolate liquor, however, is making chocolate.

Straight from the grinding mill, chocolate liquor is 53–55-percent cocoa butter, just like the nibs from which it was made. The FDA permits a chocolate-maker to correct the cocoa-butter content up to a maximum of 58 percent for baking chocolate, if he likes, but even this may not be pleasing to eat. It is hard and won't melt well in your mouth. To make palatable eating chocolate, you have to add more cocoa butter, equal to or surpassing the amount already in the chocolate liquor. (There will be more cocoa butter added to milk chocolate than to dark chocolate.) The other ingredients—sugar and milk, if milk chocolate is being made—are added, and the whole batch goes off to be mixed in a machine once called a melangeur, French for "mixing machine."

At which point, a word about the milk in milk chocolate is in order.

Before it can be used in chocolate, milk has to be dried, since the moisture in fluid milk can't be wholly absorbed by the solids in the chocolate mix. When Daniel Peter and Henri Nestlé made the first milk chocolate, they had very little choice about what kinds of milk to use, since the only ones available were fresh milk and condensed milk. They chose the drier, condensed milk, adding extra sugar to make the mixture drier still and kneading the "dough" for long periods of time in order to drive off whatever excess moisture remained.

The first dry milk powders were inferior products, usually overcooked in superheated ovens. Today, however, dry milk powders really can duplicate the taste of whole fresh milk. They work beautifully in milk chocolates, and so do specially condensed milks, dried out almost to the consistency of cream cheese, and milk crumb, a mixture of sugar and milk that is allowed to dry out on its own rather than being dried with hot-air currents. If there is enzyme activity in the milk crumb while it is drying, the flavorful fatty acids in the milk will be freed, creating a distinctive taste sometimes called "barnyard" or "cheesy." It is found mostly in American chocolate. This enzyme action may occur naturally, or it may actively be promoted by the manufacturer who makes certain that nothing interferes with it.

Regardless of what kind of milk is used (or whether it is used at all—there is none in bittersweet or sweet chocolate), the chocolate mixture, or "mass," is still in the melangeur. The next step is the refiner.

Refining. Chocolate's "mouth feel"—whether or not there is a rough scratching on your tongue—depends upon the size of the sugar crystals and other particles in the candy. The refiner (sometimes called a rolling machine) pulverizes the already tiny particles to make the chocolate even smoother.

Really smooth chocolate is a relative latecomer. Until about sixty years ago, refiners were simply stone or porcelain discs, between which the chocolate paste was ground. A modern refiner is a stack of three, five, or more rollers arranged one on top of the other and rotating in different directions. The chocolate paste is pulled in at the bottom, between the two lowest rollers. Then, since the roller above is turning faster than the one on the bottom, the paste is picked up and pushed onto the third roller, which is turning faster still.

When the chocolate goes into the refiner, it is a paste. All the sugar and cocoa particles in it are coated with cocoa butter. Refining and pulverizing the particles, however, creates additional surfaces, and unless more cocoa butter is added either before or during refining, the additional surfaces will be dry and the chocolate will emerge from the refiner as a flaky powder that is scraped off the top roller by a blade put there just for that purpose.

By the time the chocolate reaches this point, its particles may be as small as 50 or 30 microns (a micron is a thousandth of a millimeter). They may be slightly larger, of course; as with all other steps in the making of chocolate, the degree of refining is often determined by the popular taste in the country in which the chocolate is made. Swiss and German chocolate is the smoothest, English follows, and American chocolate is noticably more grainy.

Conching. All chocolate is smooth as it comes from

the refiner, but some chocolates will be smoothed still further in conches.

The first conch (the word comes from the Spanish *concha,* or shell) was actually a refiner, a long stone trough into which the gritty chocolate liquor and sugar mass was poured. Stone rollers were then drawn through the mass again and again, grinding down the particles in the chocolate. Because this chocolate was smoother than that which was simply ground in a mortar and pestle arrangement, it was called fondant chocolate, after the smooth cream-paste candy.

Conching raised the temperature of the chocolate mass. As a result, if the chocolate had been made from fully roasted beans, it was apt to be overcooked or scorched, even as it was smoothed in the conch. The new fondant chocolate, therefore, was made with liquors pressed from beans that had been roasted just long enough to get the shells off; its flavor was developed during conching rather than roasting.

With the invention of the modern refiners, conching might have seemed a superfluous process. Certainly the chocolate from the new refiners was smooth. Some manufacturers, in fact, consider it quite smooth enough and send their chocolate directly from the refiners to the emulsifying machines, where, emulsifiers such as lecithin are added, and volatile flavorings such as vanilla or vanillin, which would have been destroyed if they had been added earlier and heated, are poured in.

To others the very best chocolate is the smoothest chocolate. For them, conching is an essential part of chocolate-making. In Germany and Switzerland, for example, chocolate commonly spends up to seventy-two hours in the conches.

Since the chocolate from the refiner is already so smooth, it is reasonable to ask exactly what happens to make it smoother in the conch.

The theory is this: the particles in refined chocolate are small, but sharp. Conching rubs them against one another and rounds off the rough edges, as it also coats them with a film of cocoa butter. Conching is also thought to break up any clumps of particles in the chocolate; equally important, it seems to make the chocolate mellower, an effect that can also be achieved by aging the chocolate. Dark chocolate ages well—it may be stored up to six months to improve its flavor—but milk chocolate may go stale before it gets any better. Conching, therefore, gives milk chocolate the mellowness it cannot get in aging.

The modern conches may be longitudinal ones, shaped like the early troughs, but made of steel instead of stone, or they may be round drums holding up to two and a half tons of chocolate mass. In either case the principle is the same: rollers or rotary arms pull back and forth through the chocolate, kneading it and smoothing it out.

Unlike the earliest conches, the modern ones have precise temperature controls, so it is no longer necessary to make conched chocolate from lightly roasted beans. However, it is still possible to do so and to raise the temperature high enough to roast the chocolate in the conch. This kind of chocolate is still called fondant (you'll find the word on the label for several European-made bars) and is apt to have a slightly caramelized taste, but the word "fondant" is no longer simply a synonym for smooth chocolate.

As the conching process draws to a close, additional cocoa butter may be added to the chocolate to maintain the desired consistency. Emulsifiers will be added and so will volatile flavorings, and then, the chocolate must be tempered. (If all the chocolate made in one batch isn't required for immediate use, some of it will go into temporary storage. For short periods of time, the chocolate paste can be stored in its liquid or semiliquid form. If the storage period is to be longer, the chocolate will probably be stored in solid blocks, sometimes as large as a hundred pounds, which will be reheated and liquefied again when they are needed.)

Tempering. After conching, the still-liquid chocolate is taken to a tempering kettle to be conditioned and readied for use. The tempering kettle is a water-cooled vessel in which the chocolate is agitated as the temperature of the mix is lowered to around 85°F. This hardens the fat in the chocolate and makes the entire mass more stable, contributing to its later, fabled long shelf life.

The Finished Product

Once tempered, chocolate is ready to be used in making chocolate bars and boxed assortments.

Chocolate bars. Plain, solid chocolate bars are made by pouring the chocolate into a machine that squirts it out, on a regular basis, into molds that move underneath on a continuous metal belt. As the molds are filled, they continue on through a cooling tunnel. On the way, they are shaken to eliminate all air bubbles and to make certain that the molds are evenly filled. As the molds emerge from the cooling tunnel, they are shaken once again and inverted, so that the finished bars fall out onto another moving belt, this one headed for the packaging department.

Solid bars with coarse additives such as nuts or puffed rice are made in exactly the same way, except that the extra ingredients are mixed into the liquid chocolate right before it is poured into the squirting machine. When whole nuts are used, they may be added as the bars move toward the cooling tunnel, so that the manufacturer can control their placement.

Filled bars are made in slightly deeper molds. Right after the molds are filled, they are inverted so that some of the chocolate runs out. Enough stays in, of course, to make a thin coating on the inside of the molds; this coating hardens as the molds pass through the cooling tunnel. As they come out the other end, a second machine pours in the filling—fondant cream, maybe even a whole nut or a maraschino cherry. Then the molds are covered with a thick layer of chocolate that, when the candy is shaken out, will turn out to be the bottom layer on the chocolate bar that is now heading, once again, for the packaging department.

*Boxed chocolates.** There are three specific kinds of boxed chocolates, described by the ways in which they are covered with chocolate.

* Chocolate, singular, is the name for the basic candy. Chocolates, plural, is the name for the candies in boxed assortments.

Molded shells. These are usually, though not always, the most expensive candies, since they take more time and care to make. Each piece of candy is made of two individually molded pieces, filled and then joined together. Each half of the outer shell is made just like a filled chocolate bar, without the last layer. Examples of molded two-piece shells are Godiva chocolates and those made by Corné de la Toison d'Or.

One-piece molds. This kind of candy is made exactly like a filled chocolate bar, a layer to coat the inside of the mold, a filling, and then a thin layer to seal the candy. Examples of molded chocolates include Barton's Swiss assortments and Perugina.

Enrobed chocolates. Probably because it is less expensive than either of the two molding processes, enrobing is by far the commonest way of getting the chocolate onto the centers.

Enrobed candy actually begins with the centers, which are set in rows on moving belts that run under machines that squirt out controlled jets of chocolate timed to coincide with the passage of the centers. The chocolates then continue on, usually through a second squirt of chocolate, and then go through a cooling tunnel. Finally, they are shaken off onto another belt that takes them away to be packed.

Enrobing can be very thick or very thin or somewhere in between. Which of these you prefer pretty much depends upon whether your main interest is the chocolate or the center. Examples of enrobed candies include Cable Car, Candy Cupboard, Russell Stover, and literally dozens of other brands.

(NOTE: Enrobed candies may be decorated on top with squiggles and slashes of chocolate that tell you what's inside. This was once standard practice, but isn't any longer.)

Packing. Once upon a time, all candy, like everything else, was wrapped by hand. Today, most candy, like everything else, is wrapped automatically by machine. Boxed chocolates are an exception; they are still usually put into boxes by hand.

Chocolate bars are usually wrapped first in waxed tissue or sealed in tinfoil, and then covered with a thick, glossy outer wrapper. (Some, such as the Feodora bars, are wrapped in all three.) In Europe chocolate bar wrappers can be both literally and figuratively works of art (the Zaanland bars carry reproductions of famous paintings on some of their wrappers), but in America most wrappers simply carry brand identification.

How luxuriously boxed chocolates are wrapped also depends upon where they are made. Most American boxed assortments (with the exception of Godiva, which, after all, began in Belgium) come in fairly standard boxes. The Europeans, however, often wrap each individual piece as they put it in the box. Perhaps the most elaborate example of this is Perugina, whose chocolates are wrapped in foil, sometimes several layers to the piece. European boxes also tend to be elaborate and may change with the season to make collectors' items out of the covers.

The boxes themselves are—both in Europe and in the United States—usually wrapped once again, in a protective layer of cellophane.

All this packaging is designed to protect the chocolate against spoilage and breakage. But even with the best intentions in the world, chocolates may still be badly handled in transit from the manufacturer, stored too long, or subjected to extreme temperature changes. All of which means that they may be broken, crushed, cracked, dried out, or spoiled when you open the box. In cases like that, most stores and almost every major manufacturer will guarantee their product, which is to say that they will replace it. The circumstances have to be reasonable, of course: Terry of York, an English manufacturer, for example, will guarantee its chocolates only when they are sold in Great Britain, where they are made. (That's not to say, though, that the American store that sells them to you doesn't have some responsibility—if you buy any boxed or bar chocolate and find something's gone wrong, complain. Loudly. It usually brings results.)

You can cut down on problems by buying in stores that

treat their wares with loving kindness, storing the candy in cool, dry cabinets and changing the shelf stock regularly. Do the same when you get home. Dark chocolates will keep well in a cool, dry place for up to a year, milk chocolates for six months, and filled bars or chocolates in boxes for less than that. For really longtime storage, freeze the candy, but be certain to freeze it in the original cellophane wrap or to wrap it in an air-tight plastic bag to keep out the moisture.

3: CHOCOLATE AS A FOOD

For as long as it's been around, chocolate has been regarded as something more than just an ordinary food.

The Aztecs thought of it, correctly, as a stimulant and, hopefully, as an aphrodisiac. They also used it as a medicine, mixing it with the ground bones of their ancestors as a potion for dysentery. Whether or not the ancestors' bones did any good is questionable, but chocolate *can* be constipating (although it is probably too rich and irritating for someone suffering from dysenteric diarrhea).

The Spanish thought chocolate miraculous. Cortez called it a "divine drink" and wrote to Charles V, describing it as a specific against fatigue, which heightened one's resistance to almost every disease.

Brillat-Savarin, the gastronomic historian and philosopher, agreed. He called chocolate a panacea for all forms of mental stress and recommended it as a restorative for the sick and the weak. So did Thomas Jefferson; Richard Cadbury, founder of the company that makes Cadbury chocolate bars, promoted the idea that in its natural state chocolate contained all the elements necessary for healthy growth. His view was shared by a number of contemporaries, one of whom wrote that chocolate ought not to be regarded simply as a beverage, but "as a substitute for all other kinds of food . . . when taken with some bread, little or nothing else need be added at a meal."*

The reaction was not long in coming. In fact, it started

* Brillat-Savarin wrote about chocolate in *The Physiology of Taste* (1825). Richard Cadbury, as Historicus, wrote *Cocoa—All About It* (1896). The quote is from *The Food of the Gods*, by Brandon Head (1903).

early. About the turn of the eighteenth century, a London physician created a stir by complaining that although plain chocolate was nutritious, adding sugar made it poisonous to the system. As the century grew older, complaints about adulteration grew stronger. Some were based on hard fact, since chocolate was at one time colored with things such as lead and brick dust to make it look richer. In some cases, however, one man's adulteration was another's pure delight.

Dutched chocolate, for example, was hailed in Holland, where it was invented, and condemned in England, where it was not; the richness of cocoa butter was regarded as nutritious or "nauseous" depending on who was doing the evaluating.

Today, questions about chocolate have come down to twentieth-century basics: Is chocolate fattening? Does it cause skin problems? Can it raise your cholesterol level? Does it have food values? What goes into it? Is it "natural"? Is the "food of the gods" really good enough for people?

Ingredients: How to Read a Chocolate Label

Considering how basic the basic ingredients really are—chocolate liquor, sugar, some milk, and a bit of vanilla—it is surprising how difficult it can be to figure out exactly what is in various chocolate products.

The problem is that everyone from Montezuma's chef on down has had a little something extra to add to the basic recipe.

The Indians, for example, used corn flour to lessen the fattiness of plain ground cocoa beans. Sometimes they added fermented corn mash, which gave the chocolate a special dash, rather like good bourbon whiskey. The Spanish concentrated on flavorings. They added sugar to the peppery *chocolatl* they brought back from Mexico, as well as cinnamon, vanilla, musk, almonds, pistachios, anise, and such esoterica as orange and rose water. In England the most prominent additives were starches, such as potato starch, used to make a less fatty drink. There was another point to the starches, however: they made the chocolate go further, increasing the profitability of each pound the merchant sold. The English also sought to intensify the color of chocolate, adding such adulterants as Venetian red, umber, or a bit of iron, and brick dust. These practices were so widespread and so universally condemned (by consumers, if not by merchants) that as early as the reign of George III there was already a law on the books demanding that adulterated cocoas and chocolate be seized and the men who sold them fined.

Unfortunately, nobody paid the slightest heed to the law, although payments of bribes to inspectors were reported rampant. As a result, in 1851, when the British medical journal *Lancet* published its own analysis of more than fifty different kinds of cocoas, fully 90 percent of them were shown to have been adulterated in one way or another. Most were colored with lead pigments and contained starches to stretch the cocoa.

While the English were slugging it out over starch and color additives, van Houten, introduced Dutching, darkening the color, lightening the flavor, helping the cocoa to disperse more quickly in liquid and, coincidentally, preserving the beans so that they stayed fresh on the long trip back to Holland from the overseas plantations.

For a number of reasons, including the fact that this added freshness may have given the Dutch a commercial edge, the rest of the Europeans roundly condemned Dutched cocoa as unhealthful.

By the beginning of the twentieth century the agitation for true pure food and drug laws had begun in earnest. It was to take some time and a lot of pamphleteering and lobbying to put them into enforceable form, but the trend was clear. Lead, starches, peroxide of iron, and plain, sharp shells were obviously on their way out of cocoa and chocolate.

The FDA standards of identity. Today, the Food and Drug Administration has established standards of identity for a wide variety of food products, including ice cream, mayonnaise, and chocolate.

The standard of identity is, quite simply, a standardized recipe. Sometimes, when a manufacturer sticks to the standard of identity for any one product, he may omit the list of ingredients required to be printed on every food product. Ice cream, for example, may be labeled simply "ice cream," without listing the gelatin, eggs, milk, emulsifiers, and all the other ingredients that go into the standard of identity. Mayonnaise doesn't have to list eggs, oil, and spices on its label. The rationale is that the standard of identity is, loosely speaking, common knowledge and does not have to be repeated.

The various forms of chocolate fall under this same rule. If the manufacturer sticks to the basic standards of identity for bitter chocolate (often known simply as chocolate), sweet chocolate, milk chocolate, cocoa, and so forth, he is not required to list all the ingredients in the order in which they occur in the product.

So far, not perfect, but not bad, either, since anyone can obtain a copy of any standard of identity from the Food and Drug Administration, Washington, D.C.

The catch is this: the FDA also permits a number of other ingredients to be included in chocolate products. Among these are flavorings, spices, and colors, both artificial and natural, and the FDA does not require that these be listed by name, only by category. The notation "artificial flavoring" will do; the manufacturer does not have to spell out the specific flavoring. Some people regard this as a catch only when the flavoring is artificial, but it is just as troublesome if the flavoring is natural. The wrapper on Godiva's bittersweet chocolate bar, for example, lists natural flavorings. It does not say that the flavorings include orange; if you're allergic to orange in any form you won't know it's in the chocolate until your hives appear.

Emulsifiers may also be listed by category rather than by name, and although there is usually some salt in chocolate, it only rarely appears on the label. Sweeteners other than sugar must be listed are artificial ones. If a manufacturer uses them, however, the chocolate becomes a "dietetic" preparation, a "food for special diets." Labels for these foods have to list all ingredients, in the order in which they appear.

To start with, though, let's stick to basics. The following standards of identity will give you a good idea of what you can expect to find in chocolates labeled bitter, bittersweet, sweet, milk, dietetic, and in various kinds of cocoas.

Bitter chocolate. Bitter chocolate is hardened chocolate liquor, the most basic form of processed chocolate you can buy. As it comes from the bean, chocolate liquor has about 55-percent cocoa butter and 45-percent chocolate matter. The FDA allows manufacturers to correct this ratio for better handling, requiring only that there be at least 50-percent cocoa butter (and no more than 58 percent). Bitter chocolate does not include any sugar, of course, but it may be flavored with vanilla or vanillin, which, if it is included, will appear on the label as "natural [or artificial] flavor."

Bittersweet chocolate. Many experts say that a really fine bittersweet chocolate should contain at least 50-percent chocolate liquor, but the FDA will settle for 35-percent. Bittersweet chocolate also contains extra cocoa butter (as does sweet and milk chocolate) in order to make it melt easily and taste rich and smooth. In Europe the chocolate liquor and cocoa butter are referred to collectively as "cocoa (or chocolate, the Europeans use the terms interchangeably) components" (kakaobestandteile, in German), and the percentage will often be listed on the wrapper. Bittersweet chocolate also contains sugar. Various artificial and natural flavoring, notably vanilla or vanillin, and anything else in the candy must be noted on the wrapper.

Sweet chocolate. In FDA parlance, sweet chocolate is similar to bittersweet except that it may contain as little as 15-percent chocolate liquor. Again, it will also contain additional cocoa butter, sugar, flavoring, and in some cases a minimum amount of milk. The flavoring and the milk would be listed on the label; everything else is implicit in the words "sweet chocolate."

Milk chocolate. People often assume that the chocolate (chocolate liquor) in milk chocolate is milder and less flavorful than that in bitter, bittersweet, or sweet chocolate. Precisely the opposite is true. There is so little chocolate liquor in milk chocolate (10 percent) that only the strongest beans are used, to be certain that the chocolate flavor will hold its own against the milk (3.66-percent milk fats, 12-percent milk solids) and sugar. As with other forms of chocolate, there will be additional cocoa butter, and any other ingredients—flavorings, for example, or nuts—must be listed, even if only by category.

Dietetic chocolate. If the sugar in bittersweet, sweet, or milk chocolate has been replaced by sorbitol or mannitol, the chocolate qualifies as dietetic. This does not mean that it contains fewer calories, as will be clearly evident when you read the list of ingredients on the label. Sorbitol dries out the chocolate, for example, so it requires the addition of more fats, generally vegetable oils, which give a distinct taste to the chocolate. With all that fat, the manufacturer often is required to add soy protein, to give the bar body. All in all, dietetic chocolate, which is meant for people on sugar-restricted diets, not for weight watchers, can be more calorific than the regular kind.

Cocoa. When you press cocoa butter out of chocolate liquor, you get a dry cake. Pulverized into powder, the cake produces cocoa, the least fatty form of chocolate. There are, however, variations in fat content, and the FDA recognizes three different kinds of cocoa. Breakfast cocoa must contain at least 22-percent cocoa butter (a really rich one, like Van Houten's best, can contain as much as 25 percent). Medium fat cocoa contains between 10- and 22-percent cocoa butter (Hershey's cocoa has about 14–15 percent). Low fat cocoa contains less than

10-percent cocoa butter; I haven't found one with so little cocoa butter in general distribution.

If the cocoa has been Dutched, it will say so on the label.

Cocoa mixes, the quick kind, contain all kinds of things—flavorings, milk powders, preservatives—but a simple cocoa should be plain or, failing that, have just a touch of vanilla, which will be noted, one way or another, on the label.

Chocolate flavor. Any flavoring or product labeled "chocolate flavor," "chocolate flavored," or less commonly, "compound chocolate" has less chocolate liquor or cocoa butter than the FDA standards of identity require. In place of the chocolate liquor, the product may contain cocoa powder; in place of the cocoa butter, you are likely to discover various vegetable oils—palm-kernel oil, coconut oil, soybean oil—any of which may alter the basic taste of the chocolate and the temperature at which it melts. Usually this kind of chocolate is found as a coating on candy or ice cream, in sauces, or in drinks.

Artificial chocolate. Artificial chocolate, which contains no chocolate liquor or cocoa butter, gets its flavor solely from artificial ingredients and should not be confused with chocolate flavoring, which contains some of each.

Additives. There are a number of chocolate bars and boxed chocolates—among them, Feodora, Godiva, Pepperidge Farm, Lenôtre, and Corné de la Toison d'Or—that do not contain any artificial ingredients. It is more common, however, to find in chocolate bars, candy, and cocoa the various additives, both artificial and natural, that we have come to expect to find in other food products.

That includes colors, flavorings, fats, emulsifiers, stabilizers, sweeteners, and preservatives, among others. Some of the ones used in chocolate bars, candy, and cocoa may be familiar to you; a few may be new. The glossary that follows lists the most common additives in chocolate products and explains what they do. (With the exception of colors and flavorings, which may be listed by category, all additives must be listed by name on the wrapper or label.)

Colors. Because of technological difficulties, vegetable colors are rarely used in foods. Instead, the more dangerous synthetic colors are used. "Dangerous," in this case, means just that: a number of these color additives have been implicated as carcinogens.

Until it was banned in 1976, Red #2 was among the most common synthetic dyes used in foods and cosmetics, and *the* single most popular dye in candy. (Although it may not be used in products produced after the ban, products produced before it went into effect may still be on the shelf with Red #2 in them.) Red #4, once used to color maraschino cherries, was also banned in 1976. Today, the place of Red #2 has been taken by Red #40, about which one FDA spokesman said, in effect: "We know less about this one than we did about Red #2."

It is difficult to understand why candy centers have to be dyed at all and, considering how quickly they disappear, why vegetable dyes cannot be used. In almost all cases (I cannot remember seeing a dye mentioned by name on a label), the only notice you will have that there is coloring in the candy is the phrase "artificially [or, naturally] colored."

Emulsifiers. Emulsifiers keep oily products well mixed. In chocolate an emulsifier will keep the candy pliable and soft with less cocoa butter than might ordinarily be required. The most common emulsifier found in chocolate and candy is lecithin (soya lecithin), a nutritious and nontoxic additive. (Lecithin also has some antioxidant properties, but they are very weak, so that it is not ordinarily used as a preservative.)

Fat. Fat gives chocolate and chocolate centers their richness. Ordinarily the fat used in chocolate is cocoa butter, and originally the fat used in candy centers was butter. In modern chocolate coatings, however, vegetable fats are a common substitute. They are less expensive than cocoa butter, and they melt at lower temperatures, so that it makes sense, for example, to use them in coatings on ice-cream bars. The catch is that while some vegetable oils—such as soybean oil, cottonseed oil, and corn oil—are lower in saturated fats, the most popular ones—palm kern oil and coconut oil—are notably higher. That makes them a bad bet for people on low-cholesterol diets.

In addition, using these oils in plain chocolate adds a distinctive flavor, not necessarily unpleasant, but decidedly not chocolate. In candy coatings this is less noticeable, and in centers, even less so. There the flavor is even occasionally the expected one.

New regulations from the FDA will require that vegetable fats be listed by name (coconut oil or palm kern oil) rather than by the simple designation, vegetable fats.

Glycerin, a natural ingredient in all oil and fat molecules, is used to keep soft candies, such as marshmallows, from drying out.

Flavorings. Both natural and artificial flavorings are common in chocolate and in candy centers. The most common ones are vanilla or vanillin (see below) and the fruit flavorings used to replace real fruit flavors lost in processing. As with colors, the FDA simply requires that flavors be listed by category rather than by name. It's no wonder, when you consider the complexity of the formulas for even the most simple sounding flavors. "Cherry flavoring," for example, may contain as many as thirteen different chemicals, including such exotica as ethyl butyrate, tolyl aldehyde, and benzyl acetate.

People who insist upon natural flavoring, however, should be aware that natural doesn't necessarily mean safe. The classic example is safrole, the flavoring that occurs naturally in sassafras. Until 1960 safrole was commonly used to flavor root beer. That year, however, scientists discovered that it was implicated as a carcinogen, and that was the end of safrole.

Acetic acid. Acetic acid is found naturally in vinegar, produced by the bacterial fermentation of the fruit from which vinegar is made. The ingredient is also found in "spoiled" or "sour" wine, where the alcohol has been converted into acetic acid by oxygen. Needless to say, acetic acid produces a sharp taste. It is also used as a preservative to protect the sharp flavors in other foods.

Citric acid. Imparts a tart flavoring to candy centers. Also used as a preservative (see below).

Fumaric acid. A natural body component present in every cell of your body, fumaric acid is used as a source of tartness and an acid taste in foods. All kinds of research on both man and animal show that it is a totally harmless additive.

Salt. Salt is used in chocolate not as a flavoring but as a flavor enhancer. Sodium appears naturally in many chocolate products, and may be a hidden ingredient that does not appear on the label.

Tannin. Tannin, obtained from various leaves and bark (and part of every cup of tea) is used as an ingredient in caramels, maple, and artificial nut flavorings. Although it appears to be safe for human use, concentrated doses have caused liver tumors in rats.

Vanilla and vanillin. The use of vanilla as a flavoring in chocolate dates back to the Aztecs. As you would expect, the demand for vanilla eventually outstripped the supply available from vanilla beans, and chemists turned to a synthetic vanilla, or vanillin. Today, vanillin is the most common flavoring found in chocolate. Although it is artificial, its action in the body is well known: it is thoroughly excreted. Longtime tests on animals have shown vanillin to be safe, and its reputation has been further enhanced by the discovery that two hormones occurring naturally in the body—adrenaline and noradrenaline—turn into vanillin when they are excreted. Ethyl vanillin, however, is not a naturally occurring substance, and its effects are not yet well known.

Preservatives. Preservatives and antioxidants keep food fresh, and although there may be valid objections to some of them, there are equally compelling reasons for using others. Not all preservatives, after all, are artificial. Vitamin C, for example, is a natural antioxidant. That's why rubbing lemon juice on a cut potato keeps the potato from changing colors. Correctly and intelligently used, preservatives will prolong the shelf life of any food without affecting its safety. In doing this, they can be extraordinarily effective in protecting both your dollar investment and, let's face it, your health. Spoiled food may be natural, but it sure isn't healthy.

The following list describes the preservatives most commonly found in boxed chocolates. (Since plain chocolate bars keep so well, preservatives are almost never used in them.)

Benzoate of soda (sodium benzoate). This occurs naturally in many fruits and vegetables, and longtime testing on humans and animals shows no ill effects. Used as a preservative, benzoate of soda prevents the growth of bacteria in acid foods.

BHA/BHT. These are the preservatives that several popular nutritionists have been attacking for years. However, recent FDA research has shown that BHA/BHT, which keep polyunsaturated oils from turning rancid, may be active in protecting us from various carcinogenic effects.

Citric acid (sodium citrate). Citric acid, a natural component of most living organisms, occurs in great quantities in berries and citrus fruits. It has a strong acid flavor and acts as an antioxidant. In candies with soft centers, citric acid may also be used to keep the sugar soluble and helps to keep the acidity of candy in balance.

Sulfur dioxide. A gas that prevents discoloration and retards bacterial growth in foods, sulfur dioxide is most commonly used to bleach maraschino cherries before they are dyed.

Stabilizers. Stabilizers thicken food and keep sugar from forming in candy centers. The most common ones are gum arabic (gum acacia) and gum tragacanth. The former comes from the sap of a Middle Eastern tree; the latter comes from the roots of a small bush that grows wild in the same area. Both have been used for centuries and seem safe, but there is no definite proof one way or the other.

Sweeteners. The most common sweetener, of course, is plain sugar, which in both its natural and refined forms has come under increasing criticism from health-food people. In addition, there are a number of other sweeteners and additives used in conjunction with sweeteners to be found in chocolates.

Invert sugar. A sugar composed of glucose and fructose; sweeter, more soluble, and less likely to crystalize than sucrose (ordinary table sugar).

Invertase. The enzyme that converts sucrose into invert sugar. Added to ordinary sugar, it keeps the sweetener from hardening in candy centers.

Sorbitol. Once eaten, sorbitol turns into ordinary sugar within the body. It is absorbed very slowly, though, which means that blood-sugar levels do not rise as quickly as if the food had contained plain sugar. Sorbitol, therefore, is an ideal sweetener for diabetics and other people on sugar-restricted diets and is widely used in dietetic (as opposed to low-calorie or diet) foods.

Sorbitol may also play the role of a thickener in candy centers, keeping them firm and chewy.

Sorbitol appears to be completely safe for human consumption, but one minor caution is in order: in large amounts (about two ounces for an adult, less for a child), sorbitol can be a surprisingly effective laxative.

Because of the swiftness with which additives are discovered and/or discarded, this list can give you a working knowledge of the most common additives, but may be missing some that have been added since it was compiled. If you find something new on your box of candy, you may wish to request information about the ingredient from the FDA.

Chocolate as a Food

Most people think of chocolate strictly as a luxury, an indulgence, rich and tempting but totally lacking in any redeeming nutritional values.

Contrary to what you may have learned at your mother's knee, or from the popular diet books around, chocolate can be a thoroughly efficient food, giving you both energy and a representative amount of most of the necessary nutrients.

Calories. If you eat too much chocolate, you will gain weight. Taken in moderation, though, an ounce of plain bittersweet chocolate (the usual chocolate bar—say, Tobler or Lindt—is about 3½ ounces) will add about 135 calories to your daily intake. An ounce of chocolate-covered vanilla creams (there are about 24–30 in an average pound box—more in a box of miniatures) will set you back about 125 calories.

Some people say that a piece of chocolate before meals can actually help you lose weight by cutting your appetite, but that's a chancy proposition. Can you really stop at one when you're hungry?

The following chart lists the amount of calories in one pound/one ounce of several different kinds of chocolate candy.

Caloric Content

	Calories per pound	*Calories per ounce*
Bitter chocolate	2,291	143
Bittersweet chocolate	2,164	135
Sweet chocolate	2,395	149
Milk chocolate	2,359	147
with almonds	2,413	150
with peanuts	2,463	153
Chocolate fudge	1,814	113
with nuts	1,932	120
Chocolate-coated		
almonds	2,591	161
peanuts	2,545	159
raisins	1,928	120
vanilla creams	1,973	123
Cocoa (high fat, dry powder)	1,356	84

	Calories per pound	*Calories per ounce*
Cocoa (low fat, dry powder)	848	53
Syrup (thin)	1,111	69
Syrup (fudge type)	1,497	93

Adapted from Department of Agriculture, Handbook No. 8.

On their own, calories are an interesting but scarcely definitive guide to a food's nutritional value. Except in those rare instances when it is imperative to get the most food energy—calories—in the briefest possible time and the smallest possible package, what really matters is what the calories represent in terms of basic nutrients; proteins, fats, carbohydrates, vitamins, and minerals.

It is fashionable to talk blithely about the "empty calories" in various forms of snack foods. Nutritionally, however, the term is meaningless, since all calories represent nutrients of some kind or another. Popularly, empty calories are defined as those in carbohydrates and/or fats. This is misleading: in reasonable amounts both kinds of food are important sources of vitamins and minerals.

Even if you still believe the empty-calorie theory, though, you should know that it emphatically does not apply to chocolate. That is not to say that chocolate, on its own, is a complete food, well balanced enough to keep you going in good health for long periods of time. But it does mean that chocolate, in all its different forms, contains representative and sometimes surprising amounts of all the basic nutrients. (Cocoa, for example, is rich in copper.)

Proteins. Proteins are the basic constituents of every living cell. They are complex chemicals, made up of chains of amino acids. So far, scientists have identified about twenty-two amino acids. Fourteen of the twenty-two can be manufactured in the digestive tract, so long as the additional eight—the essential amino acids—are available in the diet. Depending upon how many of these essential acids they contain, foods are characterized as "complete" or "incomplete" protein sources.

The most obvious sources of complete proteins are the

animal foods, meat, fish, fowl, and milk products. These can be expensive, though, and every smart consumer, not to mention every vegetarian, knows that it is possible to put together a perfectly adequate protein diet by combining incomplete vegetable proteins. A number of popular ethnic dishes—rice and beans, pasta and cheese, lentils and potatoes, beans and barley soup—are a tribute to the instinctive understanding of this principle.

Like other nuts and beans, cocoa beans contain incomplete proteins. Combined with milk, as in milk chocolate, the quality as well as the quantity of proteins in chocolate rises. So does the amount of actual protein used by the body: it is estimated that the usefulness of cocoa bean proteins, for example, is about 37 percent, which is to say, your body can assimilate 37 percent of the proteins in pure chocolate. The usefulness of milk proteins, however, is about 84 percent; combining the two raises the punch of the protein.

Fats. Until recently, it was standard dermatological practice to deny chocolate to teenagers on the grounds that its high fat content aggravated adolescent acne. In the past few years, however, controlled studies—including one conducted at the U.S. Naval Academy—have shown that chocolate is not a factor at all in this disease, and there is some question as to whether fatty foods in general have anything to do with it. (Tuna fish, another traditional bugaboo, has also been given a clean bill of health.)

Today, the major concern about fats has to do with cholesterol and its role in heart disease.

Cholesterol is an essential part of all living matter, a waxy substance in the blood that, when excessively present in the arteries, can cause a blockage leading to a heart attack. Although it has not yet been conclusively proven, it is widely accepted that eating highly saturated fats (those found in animal products, which also contain cholesterol) contributes to an increase in blood cholesterol. Eating polyunsaturated fats (those in most vegetable oils) is assumed to lower cholesterol levels. A third group of fats, mono-unsaturated ones, found in some animal and vegetable products, is regarded as undesirable because, while they do not raise cholesterol levels, they do not lower them either.

As a vegetable fat, cocoa butter contains no cholesterol. (Adding milk, of course, adds cholesterol.) It is, however, highly saturated and contains a lot of mono-unsaturated fatty acids as well. The following chart shows how it compares with a number of popular fats and oils:

Fatty Acids Compositions

	Polyunsaturated fatty acids %	*Mono-unsaturated fatty acids* %	*Saturated fatty acids* %
Coconut oil*	trace	7	92
Butterfat	trace	33	55
Cocoa butter	2	37	56
Peanut oil	29	47	18
Corn oil	53	28	11
Soybean oil	52	20	15
Safflower oil	72	15	8

*Figures refer to liquid oils; hydrogenized, or hardened, oils are more highly saturated. Note, too, the highly saturated nature of coconut oil, which, with its twin, palm-kernel oil, is commonly found in products that list only "vegetable oils" on their labels. New regulations should require more specific listings. Finally, the figures may not add up to 100 percent because some fatty acid content is not listed in available data.

So long as you are not on the strictest of low-cholesterol diets, however, there is no reason to wipe chocolate out of your life entirely. Fats in themselves are not forbidden foods. In fact, they provide a source of stored energy, insulation and cushioning for your body and your internal organs, and a number of important nutrients, such as vitamins A and E. In chocolate, as in many other foods, fats, because they are digested more slowly than proteins and carbohydrates, enable a food to provide energy over a longer period of time.

Nevertheless, you can cut down on your fats and still enjoy the taste of chocolate simply by sticking to low-fat cocoa powders, such as Hershey's plain cocoa.

Carbohydrates. Although carbohydrates are much maligned these days, they are an essential part of a balanced diet. They provide fast energy from food. Without them, you would be forced to use protein foods for energy rather than tissue building, and one of the serious drawbacks of a fad diet that cuts out all carbohydrates is the fact that you will end up eventually digesting your own muscle tissue.

The carbohydrates in chocolate make it a super-energy food, so super that the Hershey Company, during World War II, was able to develop a six-hundred-calorie bar that served, in effect, as a survival diet (although, of course, it wouldn't sustain life healthily over long periods of time).

The chart below shows how much protein, fat, and carbohydrate you may expect to find in one pound of various forms of chocolate. (The nutrients are shown in grams per pound.)

PROTEIN, FAT, AND CARBOHYDRATE CONTENT PER POUND OF CHOCOLATE

	Proteins (grams)	*Fat (grams)*	*Carbohydrates (grams)*
Bitter chocolate	48.5	240.4	131.1
Bittersweet chocolate	35.8	180.1	212.3
Sweet chocolate	20.0	159.2	262.6
Milk chocolate	34.9	146.5	258.1
with almonds	42.2	161.5	232.7
with peanuts	64.0	172.8	202.3
Chocolate fudge	12.2	55.3	340.2
with nuts	17.7	78.9	313.0
Chocolate-coated			
almonds	55.8	198.2	179.6
peanuts	74.4	187.3	177.4
raisins	24.5	77.6	319.8
vanilla creams	17.2	77.6	318.9
Cocoa powder (high fat)	76.2	107.5	219.1
Cocoa powder (low fat)	91.6	35.8	263.1
Syrup (thin)	10.4	9.1	284.4
Syrup (thick, fudge)	23.1	62.1	244.9

Source: Department of Agriculture, Handbook No. 8

Stimulants. Carbohydrates aren't the only things that give chocolate its pick-me-up power. Like coffee and tea, cocoa and chocolate contain caffeine. They also contain theobromine, a related compound that is found only in foods made from cocoa beans.

There is anywhere from three to ten times as much theobromine as caffeine in chocolate. Since theobromine stimulates muscles rather than nerves, too much chocolate won't really make you jittery. It may, however, act as a diuretic or, in sensitive people, stimulate the stomach to produce more than enough acid. (Some people find chocolate constipating; in Europe there are special "baby bars," with much more milk than cocoa solids, made especially for children.)

Together, the caffeine and theobromine can give you a nice, quiet little lift, although less than you would get in an equivalent amount of plain coffee. There are about 90 mg. of stimulants in a cup of coffee. An ounce of cocoa contains about 50 mg., an ounce of bitter chocolate about 25 mg., and a plain milk-chocolate bar a measly 3 mg.

•

Vitamins. Like other nuts and beans, cocoa beans are a good source of B vitamins. Otherwise, though, vitamins are hardly their long suit. One pound of milk chocolate would supply only about a quarter of the recommended daily allowance of Vitamin A for an adult. The chart that follows shows the vitamin content of various kinds of chocolate; the figures indicate amounts per pound.

VITAMIN CONTENT PER POUND OF CHOCOLATE

	Vit A (IU)	*Thiamine (mg)*	*Riboflavin (mg)*	*Niacin (mg)*	*Vit C (mg)*
Bitter chocolate	270	.21	1.09	6.8	0
Bittersweet chocolate	180	.13	.77	4.5	0
Sweet chocolate	60	.11	.64	1.5	trace
Milk chocolate	1,220	.27	1.52	1.5	trace
with almonds	1,040	.36	1.86	3.4	trace
with peanuts	820	1.13	1.20	22.8	trace

	Vit A (IU)	*Thiamine (mg)*	*Riboflavin (mg)*	*Niacin (mg)*	*Vit C (mg)*
Chocolate fudge	trace	.08	.41	1.0	trace
with nuts	trace	.18	.39	1.2	trace
Chocolate-coated					
almonds	trace	.55	2.42	7.8	trace
peanuts	trace	1.69	.79	33.6	trace
raisins	680	.35	.97	1.9	trace
vanilla creams	trace	.21	.34	.6	trace
Cocoa powder (high fat)	140	.51	2.09	10.9	0
Cocoa powder (low fat)	70	.51	2.09	10.9	0
Syrup (thin)	trace	.08	.31	1.6	0
Syrup (thick, fudge)	680	.20	.99	1.6	trace
Adult recommended daily allowances (RDAs)	4–5,000	1.0–1.4	1.2–1.6	13–18	45

Source: Department of Agriculture, Handbook No. 8

Minerals. While it may not be rich in vitamins, chocolate is an excellent source of minerals. It contains respectable amounts of calcium and even more respectable amounts of phosphorus; provides a fine source of iron; and although it is not listed on the following chart, since it is not one of the "major" minerals, is a prime source of copper.

If you are on a salt-restricted diet, however, be warned that chocolate and cocoa—specifically Dutch-process cocoas—are fairly high in sodium.

The figures on the following chart are for one pound of each of the kinds of chocolate listed.

MINERAL CONTENT PER POUND OF CHOCOLATE

	Calcium (mg)	*Phosphorus (mg)*	*Iron (mg)*	*Sodium (mg)*	*Potassium (mg)*
Bitter chocolate	354	1,742	30.4	18	3,765

	Calcium (mg)	Phosphorus (mg)	Iron (mg)	Sodium (mg)	Potassium (mg)
Bittersweet chocolate	263	1,288	22.7	14	2,790
Sweet chocolate	426	644	6.4	150	1,220
Milk chocolate	1,034	1,048	5.0	426	1,742
with almonds	1,039	1,234	7.3	363	2,005
with peanuts	789	1,334	6.4	299	820
Chocolate fudge	349	381	4.5	862	667
with nuts	358	517	5.4	776	803
Chocolate-coated					
almonds	921	1,556	12.7	268	2,477
peanuts	526	1,352	6.8	272	2,286
raisins	689	789	11.3	290	2,735
vanilla creams	581	499	2.7	826	807
Cocoa powder (high fat)	603	2,939	48.5	27*	6,904**
Cocoa powder (low fat)	694	3,411	48.5	27*	6,904**
Syrup (thin)	77	417	7.3	236	1,279
Syrup (thick, fudge)	576	721	5.9	404	1,288
Adult recommended daily allowances (RDAs)	800	800	10–18	(NA)	(NA)

* Dutch process: 3,252
** Dutch process: 2,953
Source: Department of Agriculture, Handbook No. 8

Carob, the Non-Chocolate Chocolate

Carob (St. John's bread) is a powder made from the mashed-up fruits of a Mediterranean evergreen tree. In its natural state it doesn't taste very much like chocolate, although it is brown, like cocoa. It can, however, be combined with fats, soy proteins, and flavorings to produce a candy that looks like chocolate and has a similar, though not identical, taste and texture, the quality of which varies from manufacturer to manufacturer.

Carob bars—which are usually made with brown sugars and no artificial flavors, colors, or preservatives—are often favorites in health-food stores, where they are promoted as "strictly natural" candy for people who want to avoid the artificial ingredients and refined sugar in chocolate.

However, since chocolate liquor and plain cocoa powder are about as natural as you can get, and since there is at least a legitimate difference of opinion about refined versus brown sugar and little real concern about the effects of vanillin, I find the "natural" claim for carob interesting, but pretty much irrelevant.

Nutritionally carob is second to chocolate. One pound of carob powder, for example, has no iron, no sodium, no potassium, no vitamins A and C, no B vitamins. It does have calories (868, only a base figure since carob has to be mixed with fats to make it into candy), proteins (20.4 gms.), fat (6.4 gms.), carbohydrates (386.1 gms.), calcium (1,597 mg.), and phosphorus (367 mg.).* Furthermore, the fats most often used in carob candies are coconut oil and palm-kernel oil, both of which are more highly saturated than cocoa butter.

There are, however, two very good reasons for picking up a carob bar, which, unlike most health foods, is priced about the same as its chocolate equivalent.

If you are allergic to chocolate, it makes sense to try carob. Like any other food, chocolate can cause reactions in sensitive people, anything from stomach aches to irritability to plain old-fashioned hives. If your body shows its displeasure every time you eat some chocolate, carob may be the answer, always providing that you are not allergic to any of the ingredients listed on the label.

The other reason for trying carob is that it can be very good indeed. I've found two brands in particular that I think are excellent:

> BARTH'S Carobar (made with raisins and cashews) is a thick, rich, milky candy. The bar also comes with dates

* Figures adapted from the Department of Agriculture, Handbook No. 8.

or in a coconut version, and in small, Chunky-style squares. If you can't find the Barth's Carobar in your area, you can order it from Barth's, 270 West Merrick Road, Valley Stream, New York 11582.

ESTEE'S Joan's Natural carob and peanut-butter bar is simply terrific: peanutty, creamy, and thoroughly satisfying. The Estee company is a major supplier of dietetic chocolates and carob products (as well as other health-food confections), and the company has wide distribution nationally. If you can't locate an Estee Peanut Butter Carob bar in your area, write Estee, 169 Lackawanna Avenue, Parsippany, New Jersey 07054, for the name of an outlet near you.

EL MOLINO MILLS of California makes carob powder for use in cocoa or baking (CaraCoa brand). For information: El Molino Mills, 345 N. Baldwin Park Blvd., City of Industry, California 91746.

PART TWO

A CONSUMER'S GUIDE TO CHOCOLATE

* Please note: Prices of chocolate are subject to change.

PART TWO

A CONSUMER'S GUIDE TO CHOCOLATE

* Please note: Prices of chocolate are subject to change.

4: CHOCOLATE BARS

There are about thirty different companies making chocolate bars for sale in this country. Among them they have managed to come up with more than three hundred different kinds of bars, from plain, bitter chocolate to pistachio cream.

As you begin to eat your way through the list, however, you will notice that they fall rather naturally into several categories, with rather well-defined characteristics that pretty much depend upon where the bars were made.

Swiss bars (Halba, Lindt, Suchard, Tobler) offer the widest variety; enough, in fact, to allow a clutch of them to stand in nicely for a box of fancy, assorted chocolates. There are solid bars, bars with whole nuts, nut chips, coffee- and liquor-flavored solid bars, cream fillings, vanilla creams, fruit creams, and occasionally, wafers.

Dark Swiss chocolate ranges in taste and texture all the way from the flat, dry, extrabittersweet to a semisweet with cream that turns out to be a mellow, darker-than-usual milk chocolate.

As for the plain Swiss milk-chocolate bar, it is unique, a symphony of flavors that many chocolate people call "aromatic." (I tend to think of it as "perfumy.") The flavor results both from the beans chosen for the blend (strong enough to hold their flavor in a milk bar) and from the interreaction of milk and heat during the long conching process, which makes chocolate bars produced in Switzerland so characteristically smooth.

German bars (Feodora, Sarotti, Sprengel) are also smooth, but the easiest way to identify them is by their richness. They have a characteristically high fat content that gives them a texture some people think of as oily. German milk chocol[illegible] isn't always as aromatic as the Swiss (although some b[illegible] may be), and it can, because of its high fat content[illegible] times be extremely bland, a real baby's bar.

English chocolate bars (Cadbury) taste like Englis[illegible] late in general. The dark is very sweet and rich, the[illegible] equally rich, but milky and bland.

Italian chocolate bars available in this country (Peru[illegible] run a poor second to the elaborately made and packag[illegible] Italian chocolate assortments. The bars are smooth, but dry and not particularly delicate in flavor.

Belgian bars (Côte d'Or, Godiva) are good and thick. The chocolate isn't as sweet as the Swiss, and it is drier. It is much less fatty than any German chocolate bar, too, and though the Belgian dark chocolate is well-flavored, the milk seems bland to my taste.

Dutch bars come in two different tastes and textures. There is a bland, soothing milk chocolate and a quite sweet, mild dark (Zaanland), or a powdery milk and dark chocolate, with a hint of cocoa in the taste (Droste, Van Houten).

Finnish bars, at least the ones available in this country (Chymos, Panda), are delightful, made with a good, sweet dark chocolate. Their most exciting feature is the semiliquid fruit center, a national specialty that comes tantalizingly close to catching the acid tang of real fruit.

Irish bars I've found (Willwood) are a gritty, very basic kind of chocolate, with strong flavorings; dark, light—and whiskey.

Latin-American bars (Cortés, Goya, Menier) aren't really meant for eating. They are actually drinking chocolate hardened into bars (or round tablets, like Ibarra), incredibly sweet and gritty when you chew them, but magnificent chocolate when melted down and whipped into hot chocolate. (See Chapter 6.)

American bars (Baker, Barton, Ghirardelli, Hershey, Maillard, Nestlé, and Pennsylvania Dutch), like everything else in this country, represent a dozen different traditions.

The only distinctively American taste was created by Hershey with its sweet, gritty dark chocolate (far too sandy for European tastes), and its milk chocolate, whose flavor derives from the special taste of naturally dried milk crumb. Ghirardelli's health-food bars are American, too, with the chocolate holding everything from sesame seeds to that all-American adult baby food, Granola.

How to Measure Quality

No matter where it's made, a really good chocolate bar should meet a number of widely accepted standards of quality.

1. The bar should be glossy when you open the wrapper. (A milk bar will have less of a hard shine than a dark-chocolate bar.) A "bloom" on the chocolate doesn't necessarily mean that the bar is stale, but it does show that the candy has been through a number of extreme temperature changes, which have brought the cocoa butter to the surface and left it there to dry into a dull gray or whitish film. A bar that is merely dull may be stale, or it may not have enough cocoa butter in it to make it gleam. Either way, you may find it dry tasting and, perhaps, unpalatable. (I add that qualifying "perhaps" because there are people who like their chocolate slightly stale. They say it adds a certain firmness to the texture and, in combination bars, makes the ingredients crisper.)

2. The bar should smell fresh. The aroma you get should be chocolate, which is moist and fragrant, rather than cocoa, which is dry and powdery.

3. When you break the bar into pieces, it should separate clean, without crumbling. A crumbled bar is either stale or dry. One exception: a bar that's been left in the refrigerator may, if broken without being brought to room temperature, splinter a bit. The splinters, however,

should be well-defined, not dusty and obviously stale.

4. The chocolate should melt quickly and evenly on your tongue without leaving any dry lumps. Here the exception might well be an extrabittersweet bar. These are often drier than most others and will melt more slowly. They will, however, melt evenly.

In addition to these basics, which are more or less universally accepted by connoisseur and amateur alike, there is also the question of "mouth feel," or texture—that is, how the chocolate feels on your tongue.

Here the experts and the amateurs often part company.

A serious chocolate person will tell you that fine chocolate should be smooth, without the grit or sandiness caused by sugar particles that have remained large enough to irritate the tongue. These particles can be sheared, smoothed, and coated during the refining and conching processes, but conching—which is the only way to get the extra-smooth Swiss chocolates—is expensive, and in countries where the tradition does not necessarily dictate an extra-smooth chocolate, manufacturers make no bones about cutting costs by cutting conching time. In Switzerland, for example, fine chocolate is conched for up to seventy-two hours. In the United States conching rarely lasts longer than eighteen hours, and sometimes doesn't take place at all.

Many consumers don't even mind the difference.

Like most of my friends, I grew up on Hershey bars, specifically Hershey's Special Dark, a thick, gritty, bittersweet bar with a rough but distinctive mouth feel and a strong aftertaste.

It took me quite a while to get to appreciate the gentle smoothness of a Swiss fondant (conched) bar, and I still have a hard time of it with one of the extremely smooth, extremely rich Cadbury or Sarotti dark-chocolate bars.

If you're a fan of Hershey's slightly gritty sweetness, it's simply a waste of time to try to go cold turkey to one of the very smooth, very much richer Swiss or German bars. The contrast is just too great to enjoy without some step inbetween, which is why it may be sensible to take a short detour to Baker's German Sweet Chocolate, a bar that is less gritty than Hershey's, but still a bit sandy and about the same sweetness and general flavor as the Special Dark. From there, you can move to a smooth, but not terribly rich Swiss bittersweet. Tobler's Tradition is a good example.

Afterward, you may revert to Hershey's—it's so more challenging to the tongue and teeth—but at least you will have given yourself a fighting chance to see if you enjoy the "better" bars.

There's a different question of texture when it comes to milk-chocolate bars. It's called chewiness. A chewy milk-chocolate bar has a higher-than-average proportion of milk powder and, consequently, a lower-than-average proportion of cocoa butter. It tastes more like fudge than chocolate, and some people like it that way. According to the experts, though, chewy chocolate isn't truly fine quality.

How Much Should a Chocolate Bar Cost?

It's natural to associate higher cost with higher quality, but with chocolate bars, as with so many other "luxury" products, there are a number of other factors to consider.

First, there is the question of where the bar comes from. As a general rule, though not an invariable one, imported bars cost more than bars made in this country. Second, there is the question of where the bar is sold. I bought a Maillard bar at Macy's in New York for 80¢, for example, and then found the same bar selling for $1.50 at a specialty food shop in midtown. Finally, there is the very real question of what *you* consider quality. If your idea of a really great bar is a gritty, bittersweet one at 10¢ an ounce, then all the experts and standards in the world aren't going to make you believe that a smoother, richer bar at 40¢ an ounce is worth the price.

The following table gives you an idea of how price varies. It is based upon the cost of a plain bittersweet-chocolate bar for each of the brands listed. As the man says, you pays your money and you takes your choice.

COST OF BITTERSWEET CHOCOLATE BAR*

Brand	*Bar size*	*Price*	*Cost per ounce*
Hershey	8 oz.	79¢	10¢
Cadbury	6 oz.	75¢	12.5¢
Baker German Sweet	4 oz.	59¢	15¢
World's Finest	1 lb.	$3.00	19¢
Maillard	4 oz.	80¢	20¢
Ghirardelli	4 oz.	79¢	20¢
Droste	⅞ oz.	20¢	23¢
Halba	3 oz.	69¢	23¢
Zaanland	2½ oz.	59¢	24¢
Côte d'Or, Sprengel	3½ oz.	85¢	24¢
Barton's	1 oz.	25¢	25¢
Suchard, Tobler	3 oz.	79¢	26¢
Van Houten	¾ oz.	20¢	27¢
Feodora	3 oz.	85¢	28¢
Perugina	1⅜ oz.	45¢	30¢
Godiva (American made)	1 oz.	40¢	40¢
Godiva (imported)	3½ oz.	$1.79	51¢

* In New York City, as of summer 1976.

A Critical Guide to Chocolate Bars

This is where the fun starts. The guide that follows is designed to give you an idea of the enormous variety available (with suggested samplings in about fifteen different categories) and, after that, to give you a more detailed description of the individual tastes and other identifying characteristics of more than thirty different brands of chocolate bars, both foreign and American.

To make it more convenient, I've divided the guide into

two parts; a sampling of chocolate bars first and a critical discussion, alphabetically, by brand, afterward.

All the product evaluations are based on how the chocolate tastes to me. Since the sense of taste is as individual as any other, you may find yourself with a different appraisal: a candy which seems very sweet to me may seem only mildly so to you. Comparisions, however—which products are at the sweeter end of the line and which at the more bitter—certainly ought to hold.

A SUGGESTED SAMPLING

There are about sixteen broad categories of chocolate bars from the most basic, bitter chocolate, to the most paradoxical, dietetic.

In between are sweet-chocolate bars, milk-chocolate bars, cream-filled bars (including one in which the cream is made of yogurt), at least ten different kinds of nut bars, fruit bars, and bars flavored with the Demon Rum.

The sampler will give you an idea of exactly what to look for in each category. The suggested samples have been chosen to give you a number of contrasting types within each category—a semiliquid fruit center contrasting with a cream-filled center, for example; a nut cream with whole roasted nuts.

From time to time new bars are introduced on the market. You may come across one that's not yet on this list. Add it, by all means. All you have to gain is pleasure.

Bitter chocolate. There is no sweetener at all in this one, just plain chocolate liquor with some extra cocoa butter added.

Baker's Unsweetened Chocolate (American)

Extrabittersweet, bittersweet, semisweet, and sweet. The labels will give you some clue as to the relative sweetness of the chocolate, but given the individuality of taste, labels alone aren't an infallible guide. The bittersweet bar from World's Finest, for example, is more nearly an extrabittersweet, as far as I am concerned, and Zaanland's semisweet is sweeter than any dark chocolate I've tasted, with the possible exception of Cadbury's Dark Delight. Look for the degree of sweetness and the texture you prefer, with no bitter aftertaste.

Extrabittersweet

Côte d'Or Extra Dry (Belgian)
Feodora Edel Bitter (German)
Tobler Extrabittersweet (Swiss)
World's Finest (American)

Bittersweet

Barton's (Swiss-American)
Halba Cremant (Swiss)
Perugina Luisa (Italian)

Sweet

Baker's German Sweet (American)
Cadbury Dark Delight (English)
Hershey Special Dark (American)
Zaanland Semisweet (Dutch)

Dark milk chocolate. It looks like bittersweet or sweet chocolate, and it may even be called that on the label, but this one has milk or cream in it. The taste is richer, naturally, with less of a bite.

Suchard De Luxe (Swiss)
Van Houten Semisweet (Dutch)

Milk chocolate. Too simple a name, really, for so complex a category. Milk chocolate will vary in taste depending upon the country in which it was made and the company that made it. The sample list below is chosen to give you a taste of a number of different varieties, including a bland, milky bar (Zaanland), a bland but flavored bar (Cadbury), a "barnyard" bar (Hershey), and a pair of aromatic Swiss bars (Nestlé and Tobler). Look for good color and a smooth, easy-melting chocolate.

Cadbury (English)
Côte d'Or (Belgian)
Droste (Dutch)
Hershey (American)
Nestlé (Swiss-American)
Tobler (Swiss)
Sarotti (German)
Zaanland (Dutch)

White chocolate. This is pure cocoa butter, with sugar and milk. The taste to look for is milky and sweet, something like the palest possible milk chocolate you can imagine.

Pennsylvania Dutch Ivory Candy (American)
Tobler Narcisse (Swiss)

Fruits and nuts. Look for a good contrast between the sweet (or bitter) fruit, which should taste fresh and chewy, and the saltiness of fresh, crunchy nuts.

Chunky (American)
Halba Les Noix (Swiss)

Nuts. The variety here is enormous. There are all kinds, from almonds to pistachios, cream-filled, whole nuts, broken pieces. The creams should be well-flavored; the nut pieces should be crunchy, salty, and fresh.

almonds

Sprengel Mandeltruffel [cream-filled] (German)
World's Finest [whole roasted almonds in dark or milk chocolate] (American)

coconut

Cadbury Coconut [cream-filled] (English)
Ghirardelli Fiji Coconut [shreds] (American)

hazelnuts

Godiva [cream-filled, imported] (Belgian)
Suchard Milka Noisettes (Swiss)

Macadamia nuts

Ghirardelli (American)

peanuts

Goober (American)
Mr. Goodbar (American)

peanut brittle

Sarotti Krokant (German)

pecans

Pennsylvania Dutch (American)

pistachios

Côte d'Or Pistache [cream-filled] (Belgian)
Lindt Pistache [whole nuts] (Swiss)

Fruit. Once you mix a fruit flavor with cream, it is almost impossible to maintain the zingy acid taste that makes strawberries, raspberries, and lemon so refreshing. The cream-filled bars tend to be rather sweet and bland. The superlative semiliquid fillings in Finnish bars, however, do catch the tang of real berries and oranges, without overwhelming the chocolate flavor of the bar.

Chymos Fruito [semiliquid orange, raspberry, cherry, strawberry] (Finnish)
Elite Lemon [cream-filled] (Israeli)
Lindt Pineapple [cream-filled] (Swiss)
Sprengel Erdbeersahne [strawberries-in-cream, cream-filled] (German)

Coffee. To my mind, a good coffee-cream filling ought to be rich and strong, without unpleasant harsh overtones. A coffee-flavored solid chocolate should be the same, without discordant flavors. Nevertheless, some people like their coffee dark and bitter, so I've included a sample of that, too.

Côte d'Or Mokabitter [dark chocolate] (Belgian)
Sprengel Mokkatruffel [cream-filled] (German)
Zaanland Coffee Brandy (Dutch)

Rum and Whiskey. Traditional combinations, both, with the rum bars smoother and less biting. As for the whiskey-flavored bars, there's nothing subtle about a good one, and you'd best be a whiskey fan before you try the chocolate bar; otherwise, you may find it a harsh, unpleasant taste.

Tobler-O Rum [with raisins] (Swiss)
Willwood Irish Coffee [in bittersweet or milk chocolate] (Irish)

Mint. Look for a clear, fresh taste and a good contrast between mint and chocolate.

Cadbury Peppermint [cream-filled] (English)
Willwood Irish Mint Crisp (Irish)
Zaanland Chips of Mint (Dutch)

Specialties. A category for candy that doesn't fit in anywhere else, but is too good to leave out.

Toblerone [honey, almonds, and nougat in dark, milk, or white chocolate] (Swiss)
Sarotti Cocktail [yogurt cream, in wafers, coated with milk chocolate] (German)

Dietetic. There is no sucrose (plain sugar) in any of these bars, but that doesn't mean they have fewer calories than regular chocolate bars. Dietetic bars are meant for diabetics and people on sugar-restricted diets, not for weight-watchers.

Barton's Dietetic Bittersweet (American)
Elite Dietetic Bittersweet (Israeli)
Suchard Dietetic Milk (Swiss)

A BRAND LIST

Baker's

Say, "Baker's chocolate," and what you are likely to think of is the package of bitter, thick squares that have been an American cook's favorite for generations. These one-ounce squares are the closest you are likely to come to the taste of pure chocolate, just as it comes from the grinding mill. Of course, there is extra cocoa butter added, to make the chocolate practical and palatable, but it's still a reflection of the real thing, and purists owe themselves a taste.

Baker's also makes the thick squares in semisweet chocolate. The package says they are for baking and candy-making (and includes recipes), but don't let that keep you from enjoying them straight, right out of the box. They are nearly an inch thick, smooth and creamy, with a distinctive, mild chocolate taste.

Baker's German Sweet Chocolate is for eating (although the wrapper has recipes, too). It is an excellent bittersweet bar, much like Hershey's Special Dark, although less gritty in texture. Like Hershey's, it is a bit dry, too.

Baker is the oldest chocolate-manufacturing company in the United States. Its history goes back to 1765, when an Irish chocolate-maker named John Hannon set up America's first chocolate mill, on the banks of the Neponset River in Dorchester, Massachusetts.

The Baker in the original company was Dr. James, who provided the financial aid and who in 1779 assumed control of the company after his partner was lost at sea on a voyage to the West Indies, where he hoped to purchase cocoa beans.

The first chocolate with the Baker name on it was produced the following year, and the company continued under the direction of the Baker family—first James, then Walter (his grandson), then brothers-in-law and nephews—until 1927, when it was purchased by General Foods, which still owns it.

Barton's

Barton's makes a beautiful, rich, glossy bittersweet bar that ranks with the very best of the imported Swiss bars. At the same time the company makes what seems to me to be the best dietetic bittersweet bar on the market. It's not quite as glossy as the regular bar, or as creamy—the sorbitol used in dietetic bars makes them drier—but it's a marvelous substitute for people who have to stick to sucrose-free diets, chocolaty and nicely bitter.

The Barton milk-chocolate bar is creamy, with a slightly aromatic Swiss taste, but the dietetic milk-chocolate bar is a disappointment. It's slightly off in taste and just doesn't come up to the standards set by the dietetic bittersweet.

All Barton bars are blends of both American and Swiss (imported) chocolate. (See Chapter 5.)

Cadbury

Nestlé created the distinctively aromatic flavor of Swiss milk chocolate. Hershey came up with the special taste of American dark and milk chocolate. Cadbury, too, represents a distinct national flavor preference: very sweet dark chocolate and very rich, milky light chocolate.

Cadbury describes its Dark Delight bar as mild, sweet chocolate, as apt a description as possible. You don't have to be English to enjoy it, but you do have to like your chocolate without even a hint of the bittersweet flavoring that characterizes most Swiss, German, and even a few American dark chocolates.

The sweet chocolate is used in two cream-filled bars. The first, a peppermint, is clear and sweet, with an incredibly bright green cream filling, just about the color of the ink on the label. In these days of furor over artificial anything, that may make you a bit jittery, but you could always close your eyes and think of England while you chew. The second dark-chocolate combination bar is filled with coconut cream, which, according to my personal quirk, is even better if you let it get a bit stale. Somehow, for me, that improves the flavor of coconut creams.

Cadbury's milk chocolate is, as I said, very rich, very milky. Cadbury describes the candy as the world's best-selling bar (not having seen the figures, I can't swear to it). Like the dark, it is used as a base in a number of combination bars: nuts (hazelnuts, Brazil nuts, almonds), fruit and nuts (raisins and almonds), and a cream-filled Caramello caramel that is, to put it mildly, sweet as sugar.

A word about pricing: five of the king-size (six-ounce) Cadbury bars—the nuts, the fruit and nut, and the plain milk chocolate—are made here, at the Cadbury plant in Hazleton,

Pennsylvania. The rest, like all the other Cadbury bars, are imported from England. Nevertheless, all the six-ounce bars sell for 75¢, or thereabouts, which means (1) that it doesn't cost any more to import a bar than to make one here, or (2) that Cadbury is using the less costly bars to pay off the price of the more expensive ones, or (3) that Cadbury is using price to prove quality.

The only proper response from any true-blue consumerist is, "Tsk. Tsk."

Cadbury dates back to 1824, the year that twenty-three-year-old John Cadbury opened a tea and coffee shop in Birmingham, England. He sold chocolate as a sideline, roasting his own beans and then pounding them to a paste by hand, with mortar and pestle.

The Cadbury business went through a number of ups and downs, and through a number of Cadbury hands; John's brother joined the business in 1847, his nephew in 1849, and his two sons, Richard and George, in 1861.

By 1879 the enterprise was successful enough to purchase an estate in Bournville, south of Birmingham, on which to build England's most famous chocolate works, the Cadbury Bournville factory.

At Bournville the Cadburys set out to create the kind of industrial patriarchy that Milton Hershey was later to build in Pennsylvania. They built homes and villages for their employees and, as Suchard in Switzerland, provided a number of social and economic benefits.

In 1899, with Richard Cadbury's death, the company was turned into a private corporation. In 1927 it merged with J. S. Fry & Sons, the world's oldest firm of chocolate-makers, and in 1969 Cadbury merged with Schweppes to form Cadbury-Schweppes Ltd., the present parent corporation.

Having begun with drinking chocolate, which they called cocoa, Cadbury introduced true cocoa (they called it Cocoa Essence) in 1866, milk chocolate in 1897, and the best-selling Cadbury Dairy Milk Chocolate in 1905.

In the past few years Cadbury's serious moves into the American market have been swift and aggressive. The company now has its headquarters at Schweppes House in Stamford,

Connecticut. It has a new factory (1974) in Hazleton, Pennsylvania, and a pricing structure clearly designed to place it in competition with Hershey (8 oz. for 79¢ versus 6 oz. for 75¢ for Cadbury, the imported bar).

Chunky

The original Chunky is the quintessential kids' candy—sweet, milky, and absolutely loaded with the crunchy nuts and plump raisins that let a ten-year-old beat down his mother's qualms about candy by saying, loud and clear, "But, Ma, it's *good* for me."

The thickness of the one-and-one-tenth-ounce square makes it taste very chocolaty (thick chocolate always has a more chocolate taste than thin), but the distinctive Chunky flavor and aroma also come through in the larger but flatter family-size bars.

These big bars come in a number of variations, including a solid milk chocolate, a peanut combination, and one with pecans (this last is a little smaller than the others). Each uses a slightly different chocolate formula, but the family relationship is clear.

You might compare the taste of Chunky with that of the Pennsylvania Dutch milk chocolate and Ivory Candy bars. Both are sweeter than average, thicker than average, and quite milky. Since both are made in Pennsylvania (the Chunky in North Philadelphia, the Pennsylvania Dutch in Mount Holly Springs), I think this is probably a regional variation. See if you agree.

Chunky is an exceedingly popular candy bar that, on its own, accounts for approximately 4 to 5 percent of the candy-bar market in this country.

The original Chunky bar owes its name and its shape to a candy-maker from Delancey Street on Manhattan's Lower East Side. Phil Silvershein, fondly known as Mr. Chunky, created the bar and named it in 1936. Twelve years later, he sold his factory and his invention to the Chunky Corporation in Brooklyn, and in 1948 Chunky became part of Ward Foods.

Ward also manufactures and sells Raisinettes and Goobers,

which it acquired in 1969, when it bought Blumenthal Brothers, a long-established Philadelphia chocolate company. Today, Chunky, Raisenettes, Goobers, and Sno-caps (chocolate nonpareils) are manufactured at the Blumenthal Brothers plant in North Philadelphia.

Chymos

As far as I'm concerned, Chymos' Fruito bars, in raspberry, cherry, orange, and strawberry, are the best fruit-filled bars you can buy. The fillings are semiliquid, tart, and meticulously made. This kind of filling is, I am told, a Finnish specialty, which is probably why the only other bar that comes close is made by Panda, another Finnish company (see below). The chocolate shell is dark, not too sweet, and a perfect complement for the filling. I found the Fruito bars practically hiding on a back shelf in a small grocery on Third Avenue in New York. By all means, check the back shelves in your local grocery. These bars are worth it.

Chymos is the third-largest candy manufacturer in Finland. It has been in business for about thirty years, making everything from chewing gum to chocolate. In Finland per-capita chocolate consumption is above ten pounds a year, and regular candy bars are more popular among the Finns than the kind of filled bars Chymos sells here (just as candy bars—such as, Mars—outsell chocolate bars in America).

Cortes

(See Chapter 6.)

Cote d'Or

Côte d'Or's Belgian chocolate bars are drier and less fatty than their Swiss and German counterparts. The flavors, too, are a bit more muted. The extrabittersweet (Extra Dry) and the plain bittersweet (Fondant Pur) are perhaps a degree sweeter than, say, the Lindt or Tobler versions, and both bars have a very faint, delicious undertaste of honey and almonds.

Côte d'Or has the best label on any candy bar I've seen, with all the ingredients listed, in the order in which they occur, in four different languages. Since there are no honey and almonds mentioned, Côte d'Or's tantalizing taste must be the result of an especially aromatic blend of chocolate beans.

Côte d'Or also make a milk-chocolate bar, quite pale with a slightly bitey aftertaste, and the company makes a number of fruit, nut, or flavored bars with a dark-chocolate base rather than the more common milk chocolate.

There is, for example, the Côte d'Or Mokabitter, a strong, coffee-flavored dark-chocolate bar whose flavors may be just too heavy for people who are used to a coffee/cream-mocha taste. The faintly fruity strawberry-cream-filled bar is quite sweet, as is a pistachio-cream-filled bar. Both are dark chocolate, and in both cases the dark-chocolate shells seem much sweeter than any plain Côte d'Or dark chocolate I tasted.

You may have come across Côte d'Or bars and chocolates while flying Sabena, the Belgian world airline, or in Belgium, where, according to company statistics, Côte d'Or sells about five pounds of chocolate a year for every man, woman, and child in the country.

The company that makes the candy has a history going back into the nineteenth century, when in 1883 two small family companies—Jos. Bieswal et Cie., and Lambert Michiels et Cie.—joined forces to create the trademark, Côte d'Or (Gold Coast). Seven years later, they bought a factory site and created the company Société Alimenta. The company name was changed to Côte d'Or in 1964, but the family management continues, with Michiels and Bieswal executives still in top positions.

Droste

Droste chocolate has a distinctive taste, and if you like the famous Droste apples and solid initial letters, you will recognize it instantly.

The dark chocolate is smooth and not at all too sweet, but the taste, like the aroma, is more like cocoa than chocolate. The milk-chocolate bar is crisp, with a definite aftertaste that I find disturbing. (Droste is the only manufacturer I know of that makes a half-and-half bar—one half dark, one half light. It's called Doublet.)

Droste also makes a number of flavored bars. The orange, in milk chocolate, is quite bitter. The rum-flavored milk chocolate seemed rather weak to me, and I don't really think that the coffee-flavored bar caught the perkiness of the taste that wakes me up every morning.

As I say, these are bars for people who prefer Droste's taste. If you like richer chocolate, this isn't yours.

Droste has been making chocolates in Haarlem (Netherlands) for more than a century now, and they must be doing a great deal right, at least according to Queen Juliana, who in 1964 granted the company the right to add the word "royal" to its logo. (An honor much like carrying "By appointment to His [or Her] Majesty" in England.)

Chocolates aren't the only famous Droste confections, either. Since 1970 the company has owned the well-known Rademaker's Hopjes, coffee-flavored hard candies whose history and reputation go back to the eighteenth century.

Elite

Elite makes the only Israeli chocolate bars sold in the United States. (The company also owns the Lieber brand, which, though more commonly found in Europe, is available here in limited amounts, usually in boxed assortments of miniature bars.)

Elite's dark chocolate is very good indeed—rich, creamy, and absolutely bittersweet. The milk chocolate and the coffee-flavored milk chocolate are less successful. The plain milk-chocolate bar tastes something like Hershey's, but not enough to make it as distinctive. The coffee bar is harsh, with a raw taste.

Elite also makes a number of fruit-cream-filled bars. The raspberry, lemon, and strawberry are sweet and, like most fruit creams, bland. Elite's bittersweet dietetic bar is dry and a little brittle. It is also milkier tasting than Barton's dietetic bar, but still far ahead of other competitors.

Elite was set up in 1933 in Ramat Gan, outside of Tel Aviv, by a group of candy-makers that included—not surprising in a nation of immigrants such as Israel—the former owners of a Latvian chocolate factory.

In 1970 Elite acquired Israel's oldest chocolate factory, the plant built by the Ranaan company in 1922. The acquisition came by way of merger with the Lieber family, which owned the factory and company, as well as the Lieber brand of chocolates.

Elite went public in 1972, and today the company includes a number of subsidiaries and divisions manufacturing a wide variety of foods—from chocolates to halvah to coffee.

Estee

Estee is well known among health-food people for its excellent carob candies. The Estee brand, Joan's Natural, includes carob bars that are perfectly superb—smooth, creamy, rich, and satisfying.

Estee is also a major supplier of dietetic chocolate bars, and these, alas, are not quite as successful.

To counter the natural drying effect of sorbitol, Estee includes palm-kernel and other vegetable oils in the chocolate, along with cocoa butter. The result is that the predominant taste in an Estee dietetic bar is a kind of coconut/caramel. It's good, but it isn't chocolate.

There isn't much chocolate aroma to the bars, and the color of the milk-chocolate and the almond/milk-chocolate bars is very pale. As for the bittersweet bar, well, it's dark enough, but not really chocolate in taste. In addition, it is rather sandy and soft, with a chewy, fudgy, pasty texture.

Estee is a family-run business that has been going since 1946. The company started as a manufacturer of regular chocolates, but soon branched out into dietetic products, and now has an entire line of sugar-free sweets, from hard candies to chocolate-coated and chocolate bars.

The company has been making carob products since 1972, when the Joan's Natural line was introduced; as a manufacturer of both, it takes no sides in the carob-chocolate controversy except to say that consumer mail indicates Joan's Natural bars are a satisfying substitute for people who may be allergic to chocolate.

Feodora

Obviously the people who make the Feodora chocolate bars think of them as the very gems of the chocolate world, for the candy is wrapped and sealed with the care one ordinarily reserves for something on the order of, say, the Hope diamond. Where most European bars are sealed in foil to protect them from moisture on their long, transatlantic journey, Feodora bars are sealed in foil, wrapped in waxed tissue, and then in coated paper, cream-colored, with an elegant signature slashing across the front and a discreet gold band, complete with crown and heraldic device, down the left side.

Inside all this glory is a rather marvelous extrabittersweet chocolate bar (Edel Bitter), very rich, but less oily than the Sarotti or the Sprengel bar. Feodora's milk chocolate is rich, too, but its taste is more like the Dutch (similar to the slightly musky Droste or Van Houten) than the Swiss.

Feodora's name also appears on a number of plain-chocolate variations including cats' tongues, long, flat narrow pieces of chocolate, rounded at the ends; and portioned bars, a European specialty that consists of several pieces of chocolates arranged together to form a packet just the size of the average chocolate bar.

Specially worthy of note: Feodora uses genuine Bourbon vanilla, not the synthetic vanillin, in its bars and is, therefore, one of the few companies to make a bar without any artificial ingredients at all.

Feodora bars are made by a small, long-established German company called Zuckerraffineri Tangermunde, Fr. Meyers Sohn GMBH in Hamburg. The bars are distributed here through Bahlsen of North America, the United States subsidiary of Germany's largest manufacturer of cookies and biscuits, which, to date, does not make any chocolates or chocolate bars of its own (see *Sprengel*).

Ghirardelli

Ghirardelli's Eagle Brand Sweet Chocolate is called a semisweet on the back of the label, but if I were you, I'd stick with what's up front on this one. The bar is definitely sweet chocolate, dark, smooth, and a bit dry.

Ghirardelli makes two kinds of plain milk-chocolate bars, a regular milk chocolate and Original Milk Chocolate. The latter is made without any additives, preservatives, or salt.

Both milk-chocolate bars are slightly waxy, and both taste better when used in fruit and nut combinations. The regular chocolate comes with raisins, with Fiji Coconut (a great treat, with crisp shreds of coconut), and with a mixture of the two (much too sweet). The Original Milk Chocolate is used, naturally, as the base for three health-food bars—oat hearts, Granola, and wheat germ with malt—while additive- and preservative-free dark chocolate is used in combination with sesame seeds and with soy nuts. Each of these bars is terrific, crammed with the nut or seeds of your choice, crunchy, and clear-flavored. Health-food nut or not, you'll be bananas about these.

If you want even more of a natural good thing, Ghirardelli also has your number, five pounds' worth, in fact. That's how much the Ghirardelli World's Biggest Chocolate Bar weighs. It's $18 at Macy's Herald Square in New York City.

Ghirardelli is a California company, a division of the Golden Grain Macaroni Company (Rice-a-Roni) in San Leandro.

Its history is pure California, too. Founder Domingo Ghirardelli came to California with the Gold Rush, but he wasn't looking for gold dust. A merchant by trade, he made his fortune by setting up tent stores to supply the miners.

He created the forerunner of the modern Ghirardelli company in 1862, and by the time the new century rolled around, Ghirardelli Eagle Brand chocolate was an established name. The company merged with Golden Grain in 1962 and now sells its bars in the western United States and in specialty stores across the country.

Godiva

Godiva is better known for its expensive molded chocolates (see Chapter 5), but the company also markets a line of chocolate bars. At 40¢ an ounce and up, they are the most expensive bars sold in the United States, but sadly, the quality just is not extraordinary enough to match the price.

Four of the bars—one-ounce each of dark chocolate, milk

chocolate, and one of each with nuts—are made in the United States. The dark chocolate is quite interesting, with a decided hint of orange in the flavoring. The milk chocolate is less sophisticated—rather ordinary, in fact.

The imported bars, at 51¢ an ounce include a vanilla cream in dark chocolate, a hazelnut cream in milk chocolate, and plain dark and milk chocolates. The cream bars are strongly flavored; the vanilla, in particular, has a strong aftertaste. Both lack the aura of luxury that characterizes the gorgeous Godiva boxed chocolates.

Having said all this, I am quite prepared to have someone tell me that the chocolate used in the bars is exactly the same chocolate used in the candy (which, as I say, is gorgeous). It may well be true, but I can only go by the evidence of my own taste. And my taste tells me Godiva can do better than these bars.

Goya

The Goya bar is actually drinking chocolate, meant to be melted in hot liquid, but it is the only one of the four brands I found (Cortés, Goya, Ibarra, and Menier) that tastes as good straight out of the wrapper as it does as a drink. (See Chapter 6.)

Halba

If you like a very bitter chocolate, but don't want to sacrifice richness and a creamy texture (as you do with the Tobler and Lindt extrabittersweets, for example), try Halba. The Halba bittersweet is a splendid bar, deep and very bitter, but creamy nonetheless.

The Halba milk-chocolate bar is creamy, too, with a mild flavor wholly lacking the customary aromatic overtones of Swiss chocolate.

As for specialties, Halba makes one humdinger, a fruit and nut bar called Les Noix. As you'd expect, it contains assorted nuts and some raisins. The nifty little kicker, though, is preserved bitter orange peel, a perfect foil for the sweet raisins and the nuts. The effect is rather like a Chunky bar for grown-ups, and a comparison of the two bars can give you a chance to evaluate the differences between European and American fruit, nut, and milk-chocolate bars. I make no predictions as to which you will prefer.

The Halba name is taken from the first letters of the surnames of each of the company founders, Hallheimer and Baer. The company was created in 1933 in Zurich and began as a producer of confectionery and hollow-chocolate figures.

In 1955 Halba began making chocolates, introducing the Arni brand (which is only occasionally available in American markets) in 1967.

Five years later, the company signed an agreement with the Coop Schweiz retail chain, under whose terms Halba would supply the stores with a complete line of brand-name candies, including chocolates. Today that remains Halba's primary purpose, although the company does sell its chocolates in other stores and on the export market.

Hershey

Hershey's dark chocolate, Special Dark, is gritty and grainy, with a strong flavor and aftertaste. The Hershey milk chocolate is pungent, with an extra tang that gives it a unique taste.

Together, these two flavors go counter to the accepted standards for fine chocolate, standards based on the taste and texture of Swiss chocolate: a mild, smooth dark and a milky, aromatic light chocolate.

In creating its distinctive American flavors in chocolate, however, Hershey made all previous standards meaningless, at least so far as American consumers are concerned. During the late nineteenth and the early twentieth century, Hershey covered its market so well that it simply wiped out all the competition, foreign and domestic. It took years for the foreign chocolate bars to work their way back into the market, and even today Hershey remains the native American taste. In fact, the company didn't even have to advertise until a few years ago.

To get an idea of Hershey's longevity, one has only to realize that the Hershey milk-chocolate bar and the milk-chocolate bar with almonds date all the way back to 1894. Hershey's Mr. Goodbar, milk chocolate with peanuts, showed up in 1925, and Krackel, with crisped rice, was introduced right before the start of World War II, about the time that Nestlé introduced its own Crunch.

As for Hershey's Special Dark, it is a consumer's dream. The eight-ounce bar at about 79¢ is the least expensive dark chocolate on the market, on a par with or slightly below all other brands of milk chocolate, both foreign and domestic.

More than any other chocolate-manufacturer, Hershey's owes its success and its way of doing business to the ambition and intelligence of one man, Milton Hershey.

No matter what his ultimate position, Hershey was not what you might call an overnight success. He lost his first job, as a printer's apprentice, when he dropped his cap into the printing press; was apprenticed to a Lancaster, Pennsylvania, candy-maker; and at nineteen opened his own candy business in Philadelphia. It failed, as did others in Chicago, New Orleans, and New York.

Finally, in his thirties, Hershey returned to his native Pennsylvania Dutch country, and there he proved that if he were a late starter, he was also a strong one. Within a few years Hershey built a caramel business into one that sold for $1 million in 1900, when he was forty-two. Then, impressed by the chocolate-making he had seen at the 1894 Chicago Exposition, Hershey put together the Hershey Chocolate Company, which produced the milk chocolate he had created in 1894 and other simpler products, such as cocoa.

The company moved from Lancaster to Derry Church (renamed Hershey in 1906) and was an almost instantaneous success. Yet the Hershey family never quite believed the money would last—"It will go, it will all go someday," Hershey's mother told him in 1919, when the corporation's gross yearly sales stood at $19 million—and perhaps it was this nagging doubt that spurred Hershey to use his money for philanthropic causes.

If Hershey's philanthropy often made him seem the very model of a paternalistic nineteenth-century industrial type, so be it. He built houses for his workers (individually designed ones—Hershey did not believe employees should have to live in cookie-cutter cottages), created social programs, and saw to it that during the Depression of the thirties not a single Hershey worker lost his/her job. In fact, the company created jobs throughout Hershey and the surrounding area by embarking on a program of construction—housing, halls, factories.

Hershey's favorite philanthropy was his school for orphan boys; twenty years after his death, in 1960, his company continued the tradition by creating the Milton Hershey Medical Center at Pennsylvania State University.

Today Hershey's Chocolate World is a major tourist attraction, and the Hershey company (now known as the Hershey Foods Corporation) remains a thoroughly consumer-oriented business: nutritional analyses of all Hershey products are available upon request and the company answers quickly and efficiently any consumer queries. It is, in a word, refreshing.

Ibarra

(See Chapter 6.)

Lindt

Lindt's extrabittersweet bar is, like Tobler's, wafer-thin, very bitter, and drier than a plain bittersweet bar. It is hard and rather crisp; it breaks clean, but you'll have to have a little patience as you wait for it to melt in your mouth.

The Lindt bittersweet is measurably sweeter and creamier, with the deep chocolate taste so characteristic of Swiss fondant chocolates.

Lindt also makes the usual Swiss assortment of bars, including nut bars—predominantly hazelnuts—and a number of surprisingly imaginative fruit-cream-filled bars. There is the usual raspberry, of course, but there is also an apricot cream and one real stunner, a pineapple cream with a fine, fast flash of fruit flavor. It fades just as fast, alas, but the afterglow is nice.

Rodolphe Lindt, the man for whom Lindt chocolate was named, was a pioneer of the Swiss chocolate industry, the man who discovered the effect of conching on the texture of fine chocolate. Lindt was also responsible for another major contribution to chocolate-making, the discovery that adding extra cocoa butter to chocolate liquor produces a candy that melts at precisely the normal temperature of the human tongue.

So revolutionary were these discoveries, and so fine was the chocolate produced at Lindt's factory in Berne, that in 1899 Chocolat Sprungli A.G., the company founded by Rodolphe Sprungli-Ammann in 1845 (Sprungli was the first chocolate factory in the German-speaking part of Switzerland), paid more than 1.5 million gold francs for the secret recipes and the rights to the Lindt trademark.

Today Lindt chocolate is marketed by Lindt & Sprungli, and the bars are widely distributed throughout the United States.

Maillard

With the exception of Barton's bittersweet bar, which uses imported Swiss chocolate in its blend, Maillard's Eagle Sweet Chocolate (despite its name, it's strictly a bittersweet bar) comes closest of all the American-made bars to matching the smooth richness of fine Swiss fondant chocolate.

The flavor is deep and subtle, and there's an extra bonus in the form of recipes printed on the inside of the wrapper. Surprisingly, despite its richness, Maillard can be melted or blended into a fine hot chocolate. (See Chapter 6.)

Although both Ghirardelli and Maillard call their chocolates Eagle Sweet and use both eagles and medals on their wrappers, there is absolutely no connection between the two companies and candies.

Maillard bears the name of its founder, Henri Maillard. Since its inception in 1848, the company has come to command a small but distinctive part of the candy market with Maillard's Thin Mints and various sugar candies as well as chocolate bars. Until 1935 Maillard operated candy stores in New York City, with retail shops in Long Island City. That year, the company was purchased by Just Born, Inc., and incorporated into the Just Born plant in Bethlehem, Pennsylvania, where it remains to this day.

Menier
(See Chapter 6.)

Nestle
No matter what brand of milk chocolate you prefer, you wouldn't be able to buy it today if it hadn't been for Henri Nestlé, Swiss condensed-milk purveyor, and Daniel Peter, Swiss *chocolatier*. Together, they discovered how to dry out milk and add it to chocolate so that in 1875 they were able to produce the world's first milk-chocolate bar.

Everything after that is anticlimax.

Except, of course, that, just as Hershey defines the taste of American milk chocolate, and Cadbury, English, Nestlé is the standard by which most Swiss and imitation Swiss milk chocolates are judged.

The flavor of Nestlé is light, airy, and aromatic, or perfumy. The Nestlé taste in America may not be quite the same as the taste of a Nestlé bar you buy in Europe. Even there, the taste may change slightly from country to country, as Nestlé varies the percentage of milk, cocoa, and sugar according to national preferences. The variations are truly slight, however, with the fat content a bit higher here, and the flavoring a bit muted there. The essential taste of Nestlé remains more or less the same.

Nestlé's variations in bars are fairly routine—nuts, crunch—but there is one delicious innovation called Choco-Lite, which is whipped milk chocolate with honey flavored chips. The whipping puffs the chocolate up so that a one-and-one-eighth-ounce bar of Choco-Lite is thicker than anybody else's two-ounce bar. Do you save calories? Probably not—remember those honey-flavored chips—but it sure is pretty to think that you might.

Nestlé's corporate history begins in 1866, when Henri Nestlé invented a food for infants who could not tolerate mother's milk, a product not unlike a modern Similac. Since then, the tale of Nestlé Alimentana and its American subsidiary, the Nestlé Company, has grown almost Byzantine in its complexity, as Nestlé annexed company after company on its way to becoming the largest food-processing and marketing organization in the world.

In the beginning Nestlé had nothing to do with chocolate. First a maker of baby food, chemist Henri Nestlé then turned his hand to condensed, sweetened milk. It was this milk that Daniel Peter, a Swiss chocolate-maker, used in 1875 to create the world's first milk chocolate.

Peter put his new product on sale in a market dominated by the Kohler and Gailler companies and their plain chocolate; by 1904 the product proved strong enough to nudge the Peter and Kohler companies into a merger that formed the Swiss General Chocolate Co., Peter & Kohler Amalgamated, with which Nestlé signed a ninety-nine-year agreement under which Nestlé would do the marketing and Peter & Kohler the production. (In 1917 Cailler, the other big company, joined the Peter and Kohler combine, with Nestlé given the rights to market their products as well.)

In 1905 the Henri Nestlé Company merged with the Anglo-Swiss Condensed Milk Company, an American firm, to become the Nestlé and Anglo-Swiss Condensed Milk Company, a name that endured until 1947, when the corporation, having acquired the Maggi Company and its parent organization, Alimentana, became Nestlé Alimentana.

During this period the Nestlé organization was also expanding in the United States market, and in 1936 a holding company called Unilac was created to handle this area. By 1949 Nestlé, through Unilac, acquired the company—Lamont, Corliss—that had been manufacturing the Nestlé, Peter, and Kohler brands in America and thus, for the first time, directly controlled the manufacturing of these products in this country. The Nestlé Company, the American affiliate, now controls production of Nestlé's chocolate through its headquarters in White Plains, New York, and several plants around the country.

Today Nestlé Alimentana and the Nestlé Company also control and/or own a number of major brand names, including Crosse & Blackwell; James Keiller & Sons, Ltd. (Dundee marmalade); Williams & Woods (Willwood chocolate); B. Sprengel (chocolates); Maggi; Libby, McNeil & Libby; and Gerber cheese (Swiss Knight).

Panda

Panda bars are made with a sweet but unobtrusive milk chocolate and filled with semiliquid raspberry, pineapple, strawberry, or orange centers.

The bars are not widely available, however, and the only one I've been able to try so far is the orange, which I came across in a spice and food store down on Fourteenth Street in New York City. The filling was almost ethereally tart, more like true fruit than anything I've tasted to date. I'm told that the other bars are just as good, but as yet I haven't been able to verify that for myself. I am still looking.

Panda ranks fourth among producers of chocolate bars in Finland, and despite the fact that distribution is quite sparse in this country, there are some plans afoot to put the bars into more stores across the country.

Pennsylvania Dutch

Pennsylvania Dutch chocolate bars are the kind of diabolical confections that can set all your cavities—past, present, and those as yet unsprung—twanging in unison. The bars are very, very sweet.

Take the bittersweet, for instance. It's really not a bittersweet at all, but a sweet chocolate, sweeter than any sweet bar I've ever tried. The milk chocolate is creamy, rich—and sweet. The Ivory Candy (the only white chocolate I've found from an American manufacturer) is—you guessed it—sweet.

In addition to the usual chocolate and almond combinations, Pennsylvania Dutch makes a chocolate and pecan bar. All the nuts get high marks for freshness and size (they are all large pieces, not little chips), but even their fresh crunchiness can't compete with the sweetness of the chocolate.

Is this chocolate for you? Yes, if Fanny Farmer's chocolate fudge (see Chapter 5) is your idea of chocolate heaven. Otherwise, check your dentures, and your dentist, before digging in.

Pennsylvania Dutch is a relative newcomer among candy companies. The organization started in 1952 with one item, hand-made butter mints; was formally named in 1958; and in

1965, after it was purchased by the Warrell family, was incorporated as the Pennsylvania Dutch Company, Inc.

Today the company sells about six hundred specialty items, including chocolates, candies, and the special food of the Pennsylvania area—scrapple, chow-chow, Amish pickled green beans. The brand is available in the country store next to the company factory in Mount Holly Springs and in gourmet departments in several major department stores as well as other independent outlets.

Perugina

Perugina sells a few varieties of chocolate bars. Perhaps the most intriguing is the dark fondant chocolate (Luisa). It has a distinct hint of anise or licorice behind the chocolate, the only such bar I've ever found. (See Chapter 5.)

Sarotti

Sarotti makes the most German of all the dark chocolates, a fat, rich, oily bar, very sweet and very intense in its chocolate taste and aroma.

Sarotti's milk chocolate is rich, too. In fact, all the Sarotti bars are dieter's nightmares (*dreams,* however, if you're out to indulge a rampant sweet tooth).

There are a number of combination bars, including a crunchy peanut brittle (Krokant) and an absolutely fascinating item called the Sarotti Cocktail. This one is a layered concoction of sugar wafers, a cream filling made of yogurt, ground nuts, and citrus flavoring, and, over it all, that rich, milky Sarotti chocolate.

The coatings are so thick that the bars ought to be chilled in the refrigerator before serving. Otherwise, you may find yourself licking melty chocolate off your fingers, which is baby-satisfying, but kind of messy. In the case of the Cocktail bar, chilling also enhances the lemony yogurt taste of the filling.

Sarotti, a well-established German company, is now part of the Nestlé Company's organization in Germany.

Sprengel

Sprengel makes chocolate for the sensualists among us, indulgent folk who demand an almost decadent richness in confection, luxury in every bite.

Sprengel's bittersweet (Zartbitter) is that, and more. Pure German, it is more bitter than the Swiss, much more bitter than the English chocolate, and richer—some people would say more oily—than both combined. The flavor? Incontestably chocolate, like a double-chocolate mousse or hot fudge on top of chocolate ice cream.

As for specialty bars, Sprengel makes a number of cream-filled ones. Some are only very good, but some are superb, unsurpassed in flavor and texture by anything else you can buy in this country.

The cherry-cream-filled bar (Kirschtruffel) is just the tiniest bit bitter, and the raspberry cream (Himbeersahne) lacks bite. But the almond cream (Mandeltruffel) is gorgeous and almondy, like creamy Amaretto. The strawberries-in-cream (Erdbeersahne) is a masterpiece, an exquisite replica of the flavor of fresh strawberries swimming in thick fresh cream. And the absolute crème of these creams is the coffee (Mokkatruffel). It may be possible for someone else to make a bar as good as this one, but better? Never.

All the cream- and truffle-filled bars are made with milk chocolate. Ordinarily, I'd regard milk chocolate and creams (especially German milk chocolate and creams) as a killing combination: too sweet, too rich, too *much*. But somehow Sprengel has done the trick. The milk chocolate is the perfect foil for the delicate creams (in the case of the coffee, the perfect foil for a rich, strong cream), and if you chill these bars for an hour or so in the refrigerator and then let them warm up to melt in your mouth, the flavors are even more intense, the contrasts more perfect.

B. Sprengel & Company has been making chocolate in Hanover since 1853 (the company had been founded, two years earlier, in Hamburg). By 1870 the company had seventy-five employees and a branch office in Berlin, along with a line of products—chocolate, candy, sugar confections, cakes, and biscuits—that carried the honor of appointment as purveyors to the royal court of Hanover.

By the early part of the twentieth century, Sprengel had

nearly ten times as many people on the payroll and a business whose success was legendary. In 1912 the company signed an agreement with another Hanoverian firm, Bahlsen, that provided that Sprengel would stick to chocolate and Bahlsen to biscuits and cakes. (Bahlsen, which is the largest manufacturer of cookies in Germany, now exports the Feodora chocolate bars to the United States.)

Today B. Sprengel & Company is part of the Nabisco (National Biscuit Company) organization. Dr. Bernhard Sprengel, the founder's grandson, is still a partner.

Suchard

Unlike Lindt and Tobler, Suchard does not make an extrabittersweet bar, but its bittersweet, Bittra, more than makes up for the omission. Like World's Finest (see below), Suchard's bittersweet just skirts the edge of extrabittersweet and has the added advantage of creaminess and the extrarich texture characteristic of fondant chocolate.

On the other side of bittersweet Suchard is more innovative than Lindt and Tobler. There is the Sucarda bar, a good sweet chocolate with an almost-coffee flavor underneath the chocolate (Suchard describes it as "an unparallelled cocoa flavor"), and there is the Suchard De Luxe, a bittersweet bar with milk added. A dark milk chocolate, it is deeper in color and taste than any milk chocolate you've tasted, and richer, too, a kind of sumptuous hybrid.

Suchard's Milka (with and without hazelnuts) is very mild milk chocolate, without a hint of perfume in its taste. Suchard also makes what is perhaps the best milk-chocolate dietetic bar available, with a taste of real chocolate in its sugar-free formula. (The bar is also available with hazelnuts.)

Phillipe Suchard, as the men who founded Nestlé, Lindt, Tobler, and the rest of the Swiss chocolate companies, was an industry pioneer who first learned about chocolate as an apprentice in a confectionery shop, in this case, his brother's in Berne.

A natural adventurer, in 1824, Suchard took his savings and his curiosity to the United States—then a distant, unknown country—and returned to Switzerland two years later to open his first commercial venture, a candy shop in Neuchâtel. In 1826 he also bought an old watermill in the Serriers Valley (to run his kneading machine), on the site where the Suchard factory still stands today.

Suchard's production averaged about fifty or sixty pounds of chocolate a day, a business to contend with, but not enough to occupy Suchard's restless energy. He moved constantly to new fields—captaining a ship, breeding silkworms, managing an asphalt mine, founding an iron-ore business. At seventy-six, the old adventurer took a trip around the world and returned home to write about and publish his observations.

Suchard was also a pioneer in business and industrial relations, among the first to insure his workers against accidents and to provide housing for them, actions that probably accounted for his nickname, Father Suchard.

Today, Suchard, like Tobler, is part of Interfood, Ltd. In addition to chocolate bars, the company also manufactures boxed chocolates, which are not available in this country, and Suchard Express, a quick-cocoa mix.

Tobler

Like the other major Swiss manufacturers, Tobler has a dazzling array of chocolate bars to its credit, and according to its catalog, at least twenty varieties are always in circulation at any given time.

Tobler's Extrabittersweet is pure Swiss, bitter to the core, smooth, but drier than plain bittersweet and meant for serious connoisseurs. The bittersweet bar (Tradition) is perfect fondant chocolate, creamy, with a flavor fine-tuned to fall between bitter and sweet.

Tobler's plain milk chocolate is even more aromatic than the Nestlé bars available in America, with an interesting, subtle blend of flavors. The white-chocolate bar (Narcisse) is sweet and milky, the palest possible reflection of the regular milk chocolate.

Tobler's Mocca bar (coffee-flavored milk chocolate) is strong but very sweet, whereas the Café bar (milk chocolate filled with coffee cream) does not measure up to the standard set by Sprengel's Mokkatruffel. The Tobler-O-Rum, however, is divine, with a clear, smooth rum taste, lots of plump juicy raisins, and a tiny hint of hazelnut (the label lists ground hazelnuts, but you can't find anything crunchy in the bar, so they must be ground to a powder).

Tobler's *chef d'oeuvre* is the Toblerone bar, which is a series of triangle-shaped tablets joined together by a strip at the bottom so that they form a long, three-sided bar. Toblerone comes in bittersweet, milk, or white chocolate, each of which has been blended with honey nougat and almonds. The result is suave and tantalizing, one of the world's truly great—and truly original—confections.

Jean Tobler opened his first candy and confectionery store in Berne in 1868, and thirty-one years later he and his sons founded the Fabrique de Chocolate de Berne, Tobler et Cie.

In 1908 Tobler, one of the pioneers of the Swiss chocolate industry and one of its giants, created the Toblerone, the first milk-chocolate bar in the world to include extra ingredients—honey, almonds, and nougat.

Today the Tobler factory still stands where Jean Tobler and his sons erected it, and the Tobler reputation still draws luster from the Toblerone bar. But Tobler et Cie. like Suchard, is now part of Interfood, a food conglomerate with headquarters in Lausanne. (See Chapter 5.)

Van Houten

Like Droste's, Van Houten's chocolate bars have a faint taste of cocoa about them. I found this distinctive flavor, and the equally distinctive aroma of cocoa, in each of the three Van Houten bars I tried: the semisweet, the milk chocolate, and the orange milk chocolate.

The semisweet is really dark milk chocolate, on the order of Suchard's De Luxe, but not as rich or creamy. The milk-chocolate bar is quite similar to Droste's in taste, and the orange, which is made with natural orange oils rather than with artificial flavors, is bitter but good, much like orange marmalade.

Van Houten, which is named after Coenraad van Houten, who discovered how to Dutch chocolate, is much better known for its cocoa than for its chocolate bars (see Chapter 6).

For a few years in the late 1960s, Van Houten was part

of the Peter Paul Company. Today it is owned by the Monheim group, Germany's largest chocolate manufacturer. The bars sold in the United States are made neither in Holland nor in Germany, but in the plants of the Canadian chocolate company, Comet, which holds the license to manufacture Van Houten bars in North America.

Willwood

There is absolutely nothing subtle about the taste of any of the three chocolate bars that Willwood exports to the United States.

The first two are Irish-coffee bars, one dark-chocolate-based, one milk chocolate. Each brims with the taste of strong, bitter coffee, as though brewed for hours on the back of a wood-burning stove, and each is flashy with the taste of Irish whiskey. You'll hardly end up reeling home from the candy counter, but the flavor really is harsh and authentic; it helps to be an Irish-whiskey fan before you buy the bars.

The third Willwood export is just as definitely flavored. This one is a mint crisp, mint slivers in a dark-chocolate bar. The taste is sharp, cool, and sweet, a dynamite combination.

All Willwood chocolate is blended with honey nougat, just like the Toblerone bar, but the flavors of the two brands aren't even faintly similar. I suspect that people who like Willwood would consider the suave Toblerone namby-pamby, preferring the brash, primitive Irish bar.

The Willwood group is Irish, with headquarters in County Dublin. Also known by its original trade name, Williams & Woods, Ltd., the company traces its history back to 1856. Twice associated with the Crosse & Blackwell company, the Willwood Group is now, like Crosse & Blackwell, part of the Nestlé organization and, in addition to Williams & Woods products, distributes a number of well-known foreign brands in Ireland (Crosse & Blackwell, Tobler, Nestlé, and Maggi).

World's Finest

By the time you get to the end of an alphabetically arranged listing such as this one, the available adjectives, good and bad, have pretty well been used up, and it becomes more and more difficult to be original in describing the pleasure of a good bar or the disappointment of a bad one.

I'm sorry, therefore, that it took so long to get around to World's Finest, because there has just got to be some new and provocative way to explain what an intense and satisfying experience the taste of the World's Finest bittersweet bar is. The chocolate may well be the best bittersweet on sale in this country.

To start with, every World's Finest bar (bittersweet, milk, and one of each with almonds) weighs a full pound. The bars are 8½ inches long, 4½ wide, and ½ *inch thick,* divided into twenty generous pieces.

This thickness is not an unimportant detail because, for some unfathomable reason, thick chocolate is far more flavorsome in the mouth than thin. (That may be why some people almost absentmindedly fold a flat bar, like Tobler's Extrabittersweet, in half and then in half again.) The thickness accentuates the marvelous extrabittersweet taste of World's Finest's dark-chocolate bar, and it also allows the company to use large, whole, roasted almonds, roasted in cocoa butter so that there is no discordant whiff of vegetable oil in the bars.

The milk chocolate is slightly chewy, rather like fudge. The flavor is pleasant, more like Hershey's than the Swiss bars.

But their thickness is what makes the World's Finest bars so sublime. No one who is even passingly fond of chocolate can afford to pass them by.

Unfortunately, you won't find World's Finest chocolate in stock at your local candy store, although it may be available at a few clubs (like the Harvard Club in New York, which stocked it for a while) or amusement parks.

The company has always done business as a manufacturer of chocolate bars for fund-raising, incentive, or gift programs. Founded in 1935, World's Finest was originally called Cook Chocolate Company (after the county in which Chicago, where it is based, is located). It began to manufacture World's Finest bars in the early 1940s and eventually changed its name to conform with that of its best-seller.

There never was any serious thought given to entering the straight retail market, but World's Finest will ship its bars ($3 each, plus postage) around the country. To obtain an order blank, write World's Finest Chocolate, Inc., 2521 West 48th Street, Chicago, Illinois 60632.

Zaanland

Zaanland's mild-chocolate bar is bland, rich, and soothing, the perfect bar for the end of a devastating day, when all you want to do is crawl under the covers and hide from even the slightest sensory stimulation. At moments as that, Zaanland's candy—milky, pale and tender—will make you a child again, just for the night. Heaven.

The same bland chocolate undergoes some marvelous alchemy when combined with more sophisticated flavors, turning more worldly itself. There is a satiny coffee brandy-flavored bar, for example, that beats every other coffee bar on the market, hands down. It even beats out Zaanland's other two coffee bars, a plain coffee-flavored milk chocolate and a middling Irish whiskey bar that, though it isn't anywhere near as smooth as the coffee brandy, is still smoother than everybody else's Irish whiskey bar.

Zaanland also makes a terrific peppermint bar, with chips of peppermint candy in the chocolate, and the Zaanland dark-chocolate bars are interesting. The bittersweet seems sweeter than most, and the semisweet is really a sweet-chocolate bar. Both of them, like the rest of the Zaanland line, are extrathick bars, very rich and very creamy.

The Zaanland chocolate bars are named for the Zaan River area in the Netherlands and are made at the Zaandam factory of Hermetica, a subsidiary of the Albert Heijn Productiebedrijven b.v.

The parent company is itself part of a larger organization, the publicly owned Ahold conglomerate. None of this complicated corporate structure seems in any way to have affected the careful, consistent quality of the Zaanland bars, each of which comes wrapped in either a reproduction of an old master or a wrapper designed to reflect the special characteristics of the bar inside.

5: BOXED CHOCOLATES

Bonbons, French chocolates, truffles, creams—the very names breathe romance and luxury, for boxed chocolates are the aristocracy of the candy world.

Sentiment aside, however, what really separates the high-born chocolates from the proletarian bars is that a chocolate bar tastes primarily of chocolate, while the taste of boxed chocolates depends on a combination of chocolate covering and the filling inside.

This simple difference has a great impact upon the way the two kinds of candy are made, and where.

The chocolate in a chocolate bar is really the manufacturer's signature, an individual statement of taste. That is one good reason why most of the chocolate used in chocolate bars is made, right from the bean, by the company that makes and markets the bars.

Boxed chocolates depend upon a number of things for their particular taste signature—the thickness of the chocolate coating, whether it is enrobing or a molded shell, the kinds and varieties of centers and how they are made.

As a result, many of the companies that make boxed chocolates don't make their own chocolate from the bean. (Whitman is a major exception in this country, and a few European companies do make their own candy coatings.) Instead, they buy their chocolate in large bars from industrial chocolate-makers, companies such as Ambrosia and Hooton (subsidiaries of W. R. Grace), Guittard (a West Coast company, the oldest privately owned chocolate-maker in America), and Nestlé (all of whose dark chocolate, with the exception of that used in baking chips, goes to other manufacturers).

You might reasonably assume that this would lead to all chocolate coatings tasting pretty much alike, but this is by no means the case.

To begin with, a maker of boxed chocolates can request a specific blend in the chocolate it buys from an industrial maker. Further, there is nothing to prevent the candy-maker from mixing the chocolates he buys from a number of companies. Barton's, for example, uses both imported Swiss chocolate (from its affiliate in Lugano) and chocolate from an American manufacturer, and by blending the two is able to achieve its own distinctive taste. And though Russell Stover, Fanny Farmer, and Candy Cupboard may all, at one time or another, use one or more of the same suppliers, the way in which they combine their ingredients makes for quite obvious differences in flavor and texture.

Judging Quality in Boxed Chocolates

As with chocolate bars, there are a few basic guidelines in judging quality in boxed chocolates.

First of all, the chocolate should look glossy and smell fresh. Fine boxed chocolates should have a shine to them, undisturbed by an grayish bloom, which shows the candy has been through a number of temperature changes and may have been badly handled and stored. Most chocolates are put into the boxes by hand, so watch out for fingermarks, smudges, or any general messiness in packing or handling.

When you open a box of good candy, you should get an immediate aroma of chocolate. A dry, powdery, cocoa smell means that the chocolates aren't quite top-drawer, although it does not necessarily mean that they are stale. There should also be the distinct aromas of fruit, nuts, and all the subtle perfumes that make up the ingredients in a box of assorted chocolates, but there should be absolutely nothing musty and no off odors. If there are, take the candy back.

In many cases a really good box of chocolates will include a manufacturer's guarantee, promising to replace the box you've bought if it is full of cracked and broken pieces. Obviously, these guarantees have to be reasonable—Terry of York, for example, will replace only chocolates sold in the British Isles, where they were made. It's difficult to guarantee chocolates against the rigors of a transatlantic crossing, but even guarantees with limits show a maker's concern for his customers.

Finally, there is the question of the way in which the chocolate coating is applied. You will find passionate partisans on both sides of the issue, but the truth is that good chocolates may be either enrobed or made with molded shells. The shells are, naturally, apt to be more expensive; they are made in two pieces and then joined and filled (or filled and joined). In addition, molded shells are usually thicker than enrobed coatings (they almost have to be, to hold their shape), and thus they give you a more luxurious taste of chocolate before dissolving to allow the center through.

Nevertheless, a well-made enrobing—Russell Stover comes quickly to mind—can be thick and firm, so the choice between the two processes has to be mostly a matter of personal choice.

One process, however, that it may be well to avoid is the hand-dipping done in small chocolate shops. Hand-dipping, which generally means picking up a center and actually dipping it by hand into a chocolate bath,* was once a sign of special care in chocolate-making, since the individually controlled dipping could ensure a thick chocolate coating. Nowadays, any clever engineer can create a machine that will coat the center to any thickness the manufacturer desires, so there is little to recommend the hand process, which can expose the candy to bacterial contamination.

*Occasionally, "hand-dipping" may mean picking the center up with a fork.

How Much Should Fine Chocolates Cost?

As with chocolate bars, the price of fine chocolates varies, but here the range is much greater. My particular favorite among the American chocolates, Cable Car, sells for about $3.25 a pound. A superlative imported assortment such as Corné de la Toison d'Or, however, can go as high as $9.50 a pound, and an exorbitant one such as Lenôtre can set you back as much as $18 a pound.

Is it worth it? That depends.

Nothing is more individual than taste. Given the fact that you will pick a company that is careful about ingredients—and most are—you should let your tastes and preferences influence how much you should spend. There is no doubt, for instance, that Lenôtre's cream fillings are superb; silky, light, and almost liquid in the mouth. But if your particular thing is a chewy caramel, or a nougat with nuts so crunchy that it gives your teeth something to hold on to, then what Lenôtre is charging for isn't what you want.

No matter which taste you prefer, however, always be certain that you are getting the candy you want at the lowest possible price.

A number of candy companies put their brand names on boxes of other manufacturers' products. In some cases the seller's markup in such an arrangement can be as high as 100 percent. How can you tell if that's the case with your favorite? Read the label. If it says, "Distributed by [brand name]," that means that the company whose name is on the box didn't make the candy. Had they done so, the label would read, "Manufactured [or made by] [brand name]."

Don't be shy about writing to the company that is doing the distributing, since finding out the name of the original manufacturer can cut pennies or even dollars off the price.

What's Inside—
A Glossary of Fillings

It may surprise you to learn that the big difference between candy centers as disparate as fondant creams and caramels has very little to do with the ingredients. Almost all the fillings in a box of assorted chocolates, from marzipan to marshmallows, are made of some kind of sugar syrup. What makes the difference in taste and texture is the way in which the mixture is cooked so as to get the moisture out and prevent or control the formation of sugar crystals. The more moisture, the chewier the center; the tighter the control on sugar crystals, the smoother the center will be.

The following are the fillings most commonly found in boxed chocolates:

Caramels. Sugar and corn syrups thickened with sweetened condensed or evaporated milk and various edible (vegetable) fats. The higher the fat content, the creamier the caramel.

Fondant. A sugar syrup with more than the usual amount of sugar. When whipped, fondant turns into a smooth, white paste that can be flavored or colored any way the candymaker chooses. Fondants should be creamy and smooth, with no large sugar crystals; the smoothness is determined by the temperature of the syrup as it is whipped—a cooler temperature when whipping begins makes a smoother fondant.

Fudge. Although most of us think of fudge as a chocolate candy, it is, generically, a caramel that has been whipped vigorously and has had fondant added to control the size of the sugar crystals. Fudges contain milk, cream, and butter, so they are creamier than plain caramels.

Jellies. The basic sugar and/or corn-syrup mixture, with pectin or agar-agar to stiffen it.

Marshmallows. Protein (egg albumen) and gelatin in a

sugar syrup is beaten to a white foamy consistency and combined with starch for added stiffening. Nougat results from cooking marshmallow at a higher temperature.

Paste. Flavored sugar syrup, stiffened with a binder such as gelatin or agar-agar. Marzipan is almond paste.

Truffles. Chocolate or cocoa-flavored fondant.

In addition, there will be fruits, nuts and liquids in a chocolate assortment, and everything should be fresh, fresh, fresh.

Storing Chocolates

All chocolates will keep better if you store them in a cool, dry place, away from direct light. Most chocolate-manufacturers recommend a temperature of 60°–70°F. as best, but if you purchase your chocolates without any preservatives and if you plan to keep them on hand for longer than two weeks or so, it may be a good idea to store them in the refrigerator. Be sure, though, to wrap them in a plastic bag first, to keep the moisture out. When serving, always bring the candy to room temperature before you pass it to your guests.

For really long storage—say, a few months—you can freeze chocolates, bars as well as filled candies. That's how Godiva used to ship its candy to the United States before the manufacturing was moved from Belgium to Pennsylvania.

A Critical Guide to Boxed Chocolates

The guide that follows is meant to give you a practical idea of the taste and variety you can expect to find on any one of a number of boxed assortments. In most cases I've based my evaluation on a sampling of the commonly purchased one-pound assortment; where I've used another size or a more limited assortment, you'll find that duly noted.

The brands described here fall into one of four categories:

1. American-made chocolates with national distribution, such as Whitman.
2. Foreign-made chocolates, such as Perugina, with reasonably wide distribution in this country.
3. Major regional brands, such as Fannie May in the midwest and central parts of the country and See's in the West.
4. Strictly local brands such as Krum's (New York State) and Cable Car (California), whose appeal is universal, although their geographical distribution is limited.

Wherever possible, you will find addresses to which you may write to mail-order brands that are not generally available in your own part of the country.

The standards I use to describe the candy taste are my own and, since taste is variable, may differ from yours in degree. A candy such as Fanny Farmer's, which seems excessively sweet to me, may only caress your sweet tooth. Our general perceptions, though, should agree.

Unfortunately, you may have to buy an entire package to find out. Most boxed chocolates cannot be sampled selectively. A few manufacturers, though—notably those whose wares are very expensive—do sell small boxes (say, four or five pieces) or permit you to buy by the piece. These considerate companies include Barton, Barracini, Corné de la Toison d'Or, Lenôtre and Loft (by the piece), Godiva (small boxes or by the piece), Perugina (small boxes of Baci and chocolate cherries, or by the piece), Russell Stover (small boxes) and Whitman (a miniature Sampler and a small box of chocolate cherries).

Barracini

You get a good variety in a Barracini assortment, but the candy lacks the kind of distinguishing character that allows you to bite into a piece and know right away who made it.

The enrobing, both dark and milk chocolate, is quite thin, so that you go right through it to the center without a few extra seconds to savor the chocolate taste. The taste of the dark chocolate is very sweet. The milk chocolate is strongly flavored.

The centers, as I said, offer a fine variety. There is a crunchy, peanutty one, chewy and absolutely crammed with nuts; a nifty coconut that—and I admit this is a personal quirk—might be even better if you let it get just the slightest bit stale so that the coconut shreds turn dry and chewy; and a number of sweet, liquidy jellies whose flavor I can't quite pin down, although they are obviously fruit of some kind.

The chocolate caramel is well-flavored, but a bit stiff. The vanilla cream is slightly bland, but the blueberry cream is a knockout, smooth and drenched in blueberry flavor.

Much of the candy in this assortment is also sold under the Loft label, for both companies are now part of the same conglomerate (the B-L Corporation), and all their candies are made in the factory, from the same basic recipes.

There are differences between the two, but they have more to do with one particular specialty than with the overall taste, feel, and look of the chocolates. Barracini, for example, distributes a chocolate cherry with a liquid, rather than a paste center, and includes some in its chocolate assortments.

Like Cella and Barton's, Barracini was born in New York City. The company was founded in 1928 by two young brothers and their wives. From the first candy kitchen on upper Broadway (at 157th Street), the Barracinis saw their chain expand to more than one hundred stores coast to coast; the candy is also sold in drugstores, candy shops, and department stores.

Once part of Restaurant Associates, the chain which operated the Four Seasons Restaurant in Manhattan, Barracini was purchased by the Southland Corporation in 1969 and sold to the B-L Corporation in 1976.

Barton's

Maybe the most striking thing about an assortment of

Barton's chocolates is the precision of the color, markings, shape, and arrangement of the pieces. Barton's chocolates line up like good little soldiers. The company makes a number of different assortments (including a full line of excellent dietetic chocolates), but the half-pound box of Swiss miniatures, an excellent buy at $1.95, is a fine introduction. You can sample a variety of fillings—fruits, nuts, creams—many of which are also available in all-of-a-kind boxes. There is a good strawberry cream, a fine chocolate, a so-so caramel, a splendid solid milk-chocolate cup shot through with nut pieces, and an absolutely sensational fruit liquid filling that might be either lemon or pineapple. The taste was tart and sharp, but I couldn't quite pin it down. All the candies in the Swiss assortment are molded so that even in the miniature size they have a thick firm shell, either mild dark or distinctively Swiss-tasting milk.

To my mind, the finest specialty item is the Viennese Crunch, a butterscotch-flavored hard-candy square covered with milk chocolate and nuts. I used to devour them as a kid and still find them a great way to soothe a sweet tooth.

Though many a small company has long since sold out to one or another major conglomerate, Barton's is still run by the people who started it. The company was founded in 1940, in a small store on upper Broadway in New York City, by Stephen Klein, a candy-maker who, some sources say, chose the name for his company from Franklin Roosevelt's radio speeches on "Martin, Barton and Fish." Today Barton's is a publicly owned corporation with headquarters in Brooklyn, New York; sales volume places it fifth or sixth among U.S. manufacturers of chocolate candies.

Barton's candies are made from both American and Swiss chocolate, the latter imported from Barton's affiliate in Lugano. All Barton's products are kosher—no animal fats, glycerin, or gelatin are used—and there is also a full line of products produced specially for the Jewish season of Passover.

Blum's

Blum's makes good-looking candy, with clear, strong markings on good-size pieces that, although enrobed, have the firm glossy look of molded shells. The coatings are thick, too, and there is a satisfactory mixture of light and dark chocolate, as well as a number of pastels or tinted confectioners' coating. The centers include a chewy nougat and a superlative chocolate cream, but since I'm not overly fond of caramels, I found the high percentage of them a drawback. I do have to admit, though, that people who like caramels will be crazy about these: they are firm and buttery, and blend nicely with the mild chocolate coatings.

Simon Blum created Blum's of San Francisco in 1890 to cater to well-bred, demanding customers. He offered service along with his candies and cakes, including free delivery and a personal-selection file (it ultimately numbered in the thousands) through which favored customers could simply request their mixtures.

Today Blum's still has a San Francisco address, although its factory, like several other candy-makers', is in Nebraska. The candies are sold throughout the United States and overseas.

Brigham's

There is a two-inch round milk-chocolate medallion marked Souvenir of Boston right in the middle of the one-pound box of Brigham's Boston Assortment, but even if it weren't there, you'd know that this is New England-made candy by the predominance of the maple-walnut flavoring.

There are a lot of maple-walnut creams, slightly sugary but very clear in taste, and a lot of nuts, too—whole, on top of chocolate creams, and broken and/or crushed as a coating for chocolate caramels that are, to me at least, the ultimate adult Tootsie Roll, a smoother, more sophisticated version of that mouth-filling chocolate confection that got me through so many dreadful children's matinees, where, absorbed in the total chocolate experience, I sat oblivious to the machinations of Bugs Bunny, the Saturday talent show with neighborhood kids, and the hysterics from the kiddie-section matron.

The assortment also includes a splendid chocolate cream, and the coatings, a mild dark and a sweet milk chocolate, enhance rather than compete with the centers.

The candy travels well, too. My package arrived spanking fresh, with everything whole and in place, the result of the kind of packing and handling that shows respect for the product.

Brigham's candy-making goes back to 1914, when the Durand Company, one of four companies that were ultimately to be incorporated under the Brigham label, opened its candy-store doors.

Today, Brigham's is a Boston-based chain of more than one hundred ice-cream and candy stores, identifiable by the exuberant red, white, and blue Brigham logo. The candy is sold along the East Coast, and since Brigham's is now a subsidiary of Chicago's Jewel Company, Inc., its products also appear in the Jewel stores.

Cable Car

Since I live in the East and Cable Car is made and sold in California, I'm a latecomer to the brand. That's turned out to be a blessing in disguise, though. Having tasted almost everything else first, I have very little hesitation in saying that I think Cable Car makes the best candy sold in this country under an American label.

As a matter of fact, it almost knocks out the foreign competition, too, since its price—$3.25 a pound—is far more realistic than any import.

Cable Car's lead begins with the chocolate coating on its enrobed pieces. The dark chocolate is superb, a sophisticated bittersweet that comes closer than anything else I have tasted to the distinctive flavor of an excellent Swiss bittersweet bar. The milk chocolate is an equally subtle blend. Inside, the fillings are simply terrific: the creams—a strong coffee, a good nut, a tart pineapple, and a fine vanilla—are silky on the tongue, as good, or better, than the Lenôtre creams from France. There is the usual assortment of other centers, each one just a little bit better than others you may have tasted, and there is one sensational filling I haven't found anywhere else, a cinnamon-apple combination that tastes just like a freshly baked apple.

Cable Car, a subsidiary of Glaser Brothers, a West Coast tobacco distributor, has been making its candy since 1966, but still does not distribute it outside of California, where it is sold in Montgomery Ward stores and the customary food and candy shops. (There is also one Montgomery Ward store in Nevada that stocks the brand, but that's it.) If you do not live along the West Coast and would like to try the candy, you may request information about orders and prices from Cable Car Candy Company, 700 West Pacific Coast Highway, Long Beach, California 90806.

Candy Cupboard

Candy Cupboard is an astonishing bargain. While imported chocolate assortments sell for anywhere from $6.95 to $18 a pound, and good domestic candy can go up to $8.50, these beautifully made, superior chocolates sell for $2.95 a pound.

Now, let's be clear about it. These aren't molded chocolates like Godiva or extravagantly rich ones like Cable Car. But they are obviously excellent, with a quality so inescapable that you can tell you're on to something good the minute you open the box and smell the rich, enveloping chocolate aroma. The pieces are large and attractively designed, set snugly into plastic trays that, while they make a nice presentation, aren't designed to fool the eye into seeing more chocolates than there really are.

The chocolate coatings, both dark and light, are sweet but not overly so, and the fillings—with the exception of one horrendous cherry (?) cream—are terrific. There is a truly singular coconut center, moist, yet dry enough so that the slightly rough texture of the coconut shreds is crunchy and sweet on your tongue. There is a slightly different solid chocolate cup, with chips of mint instead of the more common chips of nut, and there is a smooth chocolate cream that is actually somewhere between cream and fudge. The maple-walnut cream is slightly stronger than I'd prefer, but all in all, this is a marvelous buy that I recommend without reservations.

Candy Cupboard is owned by NECCO (New England Confectionery Company), which in turn is owned by one of those faceless conglomerates, United Industries Syndicate.

The brand was first put on the market in 1941, eight years after NECCO, which had made its reputation as a manufacturer of sugar wafers and mints, acquired a small New England chocolate-maker called Lovell & Covel Company.

The goal then was to introduce a line of quality chocolates at popular prices, and to judge from what I've tasted, they've certainly made it.

Cella

Cella makes only one kind of candy, a chocolate cherry cordial that is the Cadillac, or maybe even the Rolls-Royce, of the chocolate cherry trade.

Every other chocolate cherry cordial made in this country starts with a maraschino cherry embedded in a blob of starch or starch/sugar paste to which invertase, an enzyme, is added. Once the candy has been chocolate-coated and packed, the invertase begins to break down the paste center so that by the time the cherry gets to you, the filling is more or less liquid.

Cella's cherries, on the other hand, are bathed in 100 percent liquid right from the start, when they are dropped into thick, firm, molded chocolate shells (either dark or milk), and then sealed by a patented process that keeps the liquid from leaking out and allows Cella to remain the only company in the country able to produce these little beauties.

As for the chocolate shells, well, perfect isn't at all a bad description. The dark is a mild bittersweet, the milk is satiny, and the price is unbelievable: about $2.00 for a box of twenty-two gorgeous (and generously proportioned) cherries.

Cella has been in business since 1864. The company is a longtime resident of the lower Manhattan area around Canal Street and West Broadway, where dozens of candy companies once made everything from gumdrops to chocolates.

Today almost everyone else has left, but Cella is still there, in a spanking-new brick factory on West Broadway. The reason is a lot more practical than it is sentimental. Cella started manufacturing liquid-filled chocolate cherries in the late 1920s, using a machine that is several stories high and far too complicated to relocate. "We never knew whether the thing would work if we moved it," a spokesman says, "so we decided simply to renovate around it."

Family-run until 1969, Cella is now part of a conglomerate, in unlikely partnership with Lehigh Coal and Navigation, a railroad.

Corne de la Toison d'Or

Some people make good chocolates. Some people make better chocolates. Corné de la Toison d'Or, a firm of Belgian *chocolatiers*, makes the best chocolates. They are sumptuous; slightly more expensive than Godiva (though far less costly than Lenôtre) and richer, too.

The first time I ever tasted this candy was when a dinner guest brought along a half-pound box as a house gift. When I opened the box, the white enamel paper folded back to reveal chocolates so lush and glossy that we decided on the spot to leave the sherbert in the freezer and serve the candy for dessert instead.

There were four of us that night, chocolate-lovers all, with better-than-average appetites. Nevertheless, we simply couldn't finish the box. Two, maybe three pieces each, but no more. That's how incredibly rich the candy was.

From the thick, molded-chocolate shell—the company makes its own chocolate, right from the bean—through creams, nougats, and the like, Corné de la Toison d'Or is imaginative, sophisticated, and suave. There are no preservatives, no artificial anything. All there is, is pleasure.

Corné de la Toison d'Or was founded in Brussels in 1936 and has been run ever since by the Girardi-Corné family. They run it with a tight hand on quality. Only fresh butter and creams are used in the filled bonbons, and the candy must be stored at cool temperatures to maintain its freshness.

This isn't mass-produced candy; it's made only after they receive an order, and Mme Henriette Girardi-Corné speaks of a "mutual understanding" between serious gourmets and Corné de la Toison d'Or. "Delays in delivery may occur," she says, "but the quality stands."

The company sells its products in Belgium through sixty-one special units and independent retailers (who may sell hard candies from other companies, but no competing chocolates). It exports to England, France, and Germany, and in the United States sells through Bloomingdale's in New York.

To order, write to Candy Department, Bloomingdale's, 1000 Third Avenue, New York, New York 10022. The company ships airmail or special delivery only, and the price is approximately $9.50 a pound, plus shipping charges. If you're in New York, you can buy in lesser quantities, choosing your own selection by the piece at Bloomingdale's Au Chocolat.

Cortina

The half-pound box of Cortina chocolates retails for a dollar and some very small change. The quality of the candy, while not deluxe, is quite good.

One reason for the low price may well be that there are only a limited number of centers: cherry cordials, a really good chocolate fudge, caramels, a super coconut cream, and a fair vanilla (three pieces of each). The limited variety hasn't limited the high-priced ingredients. Cortina's label lists all the good stuff—heavy cream, assorted nuts, honey, butter, coconut, and cherries.

The chocolate coating is slightly sugary, but nicely flavored.

There are two company names on the Cortina box, Welch's and Nabisco. The brand name was originally owned by the James O. Welch Company of Boston, which twenty years ago was assimilated by Nabisco. The candy is now made by Nabisco Confections, Inc. The chocolate coating is made by another Nabisco division, Mercken's, a large coating manufacturer in Boston.

Droste

Droste is medium-priced candy ($5.95 for the fourteen-ounce Royal Assortment) both molded chocolates and enrobed ones. The chocolate is faintly cocoa-tasting like the Droste candy bars. (There is one knockout eggnog cream in dark chocolate). The Droste apples and initials (large and small solid-chocolate letters) are much better known, however, and more widely available than the chocolates. Both make nice-looking presents all year round, although, you may find the chocolate a bit too powdery. (See Droste in Chapters 4 and 6.)

Elite

Elite makes the only brands of Israeli boxed chocolates sold in this country* and should definitely be part of your taste-testing. The chocolates are individually wrapped in colored foil, like Perugina's, although the foils are not nearly so elaborate as those on the Italian chocolates.

The taste of the chocolate is rather like that of the Elite chocolate bars, though slightly more caramel. The pieces have a good thick bottom; nearly half the piece, in fact, is made up of the chocolate underside. The candies look molded, although they are not shells, and have the nice, precise look of Barton's chocolates.

Unfortunately, because the chocolates have so far to travel, the quality may vary from box to box. Bloom is hard to avoid when chocolates go through so many different areas on the way from Israel to your friendly neighborhood candy store, and it is difficult, too, to keep the centers from drying out. I found the creams smooth, but it was hard to distinguish one taste from another. The chocolate cream was good, but the fruit creams all tasted alike.

Fanny Farmer

Just saying that Fanny Farmer candy is sweet candy doesn't quite get the message across. Even saying that it's *very* sweet doesn't really do it. No, you've got to understand that the dark chocolate is very sweet, the milk chocolate (which tastes something like Hershey's) is very sweet, and the centers (all quite ordinary, except for one bubble-gum-pink filling that tastes like—what else?—bubble gum) are very sweet, sweet, sweet.

The entire sensation is something of a shock to the palate. As a friend of mine, who I must admit, adores Fanny

* Elite, the Exodus assortment, and Lieber.

Farmer's fudge puts it: "The stuff is so sweet, it sends shivers up your spine." If you take your coffee with three teaspoons of sugar, this is *your* chocolate.

Contrary to what you may always have thought, Fanny Farmer candy shops weren't started by a dear little old lady named Fanny Farmer. Actually, her name was Fann*ie*, and what *she* did was write the famous *Boston Cooking School Cookbook.*

The shops were the invention of someone else entirely, a candy-maker named Frank O'Connor who had been so impressed with Miss Farmer's grit and determination (she had been paralyzed as a child and walked with a slight limp, but had completed her education and created her career in spite of her handicap) that he chose her name for the chain of stores he started about 1910. (Mr. O'Connor seems to have had a thing for gritty, determined ladies: he named his Canadian chain after Laura Secord, an eighteenth-century lady whose bravery saved dozens of her fellow countrymen from death during an American attack at the Battle of Beaver Dam, during the War of 1812.)

Today the Fanny Farmer company owns the right to the name, as well as to the *Boston Cooking School Cookbook* and its later incarnations, and Fanny Farmer Candy is sold coast to coast in Fanny Farmer shops, and in various other retail stores.

It's a sweet story.

Fannie May

The Chicago-based chain of Fannie May shops is famous throughout the Midwest for its peanut brittle, a buttery, nutty confection that absolutely demands your attention, even when coated with a so-so milk chocolate and packed into the one-pound assortment of Fannie May chocolates.

Aside from the peanut brittle, the assortment is most notable for its use of three different kinds of chocolate coating: milk chocolate, dark sweet chocolate, and a pure, bitter chocolate over a pristine vanilla-cream center. This combination—bitter chocolate and vanilla cream—is quite an old-fashioned one that used to be quite popular. As far as I know, only Fannie May makes it now.

The assortment also includes a number of brightly tinted pieces of candy: a coconut cream in pink confectioners' coating, a mint in green. If plain brown chocolate bores you, this assortment is for you. The pieces, both chocolate and tinted, are generous.

Fannie May is a privately owned company that has been in business since 1920. Today there are shops in Illinois, Indiana, Michigan, Iowa, Wisconsin, Minnesota, New Jersey, Maryland, Virginia, and Washington, D.C. Outside those states, mail orders are available. For catalog and price list write to Fannie May, 1137 West Jackson Boulevard, Chicago, Illinois 60607.

Godiva

Godiva is luxury chocolate. You'll respect the price immediately (it sells for approximately $8.50 a pound), but you may not really appreciate the artistry of the chocolates unless you get around to them after you've tried a number of other assortments.

To begin with, Godiva uses no preservatives at all, no artificial colors, no artificial flavors. The absence of the artificial colors and flavors means the candy is "natural," whereas the absence of preservatives means that it merits special attention. The company refrigerates its display cases in the Godiva boutiques around the country. You don't have to do that at home, unless you plan to keep the chocolates for a while—say, three or four weeks—but you do have to keep it away from any extreme heat.

Godiva's second attribute is the care with which each piece is made. Most Godiva candy is molded, the shells made in two pieces, filled, and then assembled. Of the twenty different kinds of chocolates sold in Godiva assortments, seventeen are molded. As a result, each piece has a thick firm chocolate shell, glossy in the box and slow-melting in the mouth. You get a definite chance to savor the chocolate before it dissolves and the filling takes over.

The shells are either milk or dark chocolate. The milk seems a bit more subtle in its flavoring, although the dark is a good bitter-sweet balance, flavorful, but not so strong as to overpower the fillings, which are great. There's a snappy lemon cream, one of the few I've found that isn't sugary, grainy, too sweet, or worse yet, bitter. There's also a butterscotch caramel with hazelnuts, chocolate with a nifty trace of liqueur, a mild coffee cream, and strawberry with tiny pieces of fruit.

Is the candy worth the price? Yes, but not if what you're looking for is something to munch in front of the television set. Godiva is meant for serious dining; serve it alone, for dessert, with espresso to balance the richness, and you've got an end to a meal that any Roman banqueter might envy.

Considering the elegance of the Godiva product and its packaging, many food snobs often react with surprise—not to mention shock—when they learn that Godiva comes courtesy of the same people who once sponsored those chubby cutie pies, the Campbell kids.

That's right. Godiva Chocolatier, Inc., is a division of Pepperidge Farm, which in turn is a subsidiary of the Campbell Soup Company. The association dates back to 1966, when Campbell acquired the right to produce and sell the chocolate of the Belgian Godiva company here in the United States. The Campbell people bought an interest in the Belgian firm in 1971 and acquired it outright in 1974. The quality of the chocolate doesn't seem to have declined in the slightest, and today all Godiva chocolates sold in this country (with the exception of a few candy bars and one or two specialty items) are made at the Pepperidge Farm plant in Pennsylvania.

There's been no loss of quality, either, in the Godiva packaging, which, in the European tradition, is gorgeous. Godiva chocolates are sold in gold ballotins (boxes) and other pretty packages in one-, two-, three-, and five-pound sizes. The company, however, also makes allowance for the poor but devoted chocolate-lovers among us and sells a sampler box for $1, as well as selections by the piece (2 for 60¢).

Kron

Krön started as a small shop on New York's East Side. In the past few years it has built a very large reputation as a candy-maker to the chic and powerful. All its candies are assembled on the spot, in a glass-windowed kitchen next to the second-floor salesroom. This gives Krön a certain flexibility in its inventory, which has permitted intriguing innovations such as big, fat strawberries dipped in chocolate. Then, too, there is no getting around that upper Madison Avenue address and the high prices that go with it (a one-pound assortment, in a small wooden shipping case, costs $12.50). Together, they have given Krön a certain cachet among the pretty people in Manhattan and their outlander visitors.

Krön does not make its own chocolate, from the bean, but its chocolates are good. They come in dark, milk, and white (solid bricks of each are available at $8 for one pound; with cashews, $8.50; with Macadamia nuts, $10). The dark chocolate is particularly good, slightly more bitter than most other American coating I've tasted (all Krön's chocolates are dipped), and richer, too, on the order of Tobler's, which are the richest by far of all the chocolates I've come across.

The one-pound assortment includes dried fruit (tart apricots, dried prunes, and raisins), nut pastes, solid shell-shaped pastilles (dime-size pieces of solid chocolate), nut clusters, and cherry cordials with a liqueur-flavored semiliquid center. Krön also makes a number of catchy specialties: solid-chocolate greeting cards with messages on top, and solid-chocolate golf balls, alphabet letters, and the words "love," "Noel," or "thanks."

Certainly Krön is a curiosity piece for anyone who's nuts about chocolate, but with all the attractions—good chocolate, imaginative packaging and merchandising, a solid grasp of media public relations—there is still the very real question of whether Krön's candies (the second most expensive in the country; only Lenôtre's, at $18 a pound, cost more), or *any* candies, for that matter, are worth the price.

There are Krön branches opening in Beverly Hills and Bal Harbour, Florida, and the New York Krön shop does a very limited mail-order business, mostly limited to previous customers who have picked up a simple mail-order list from the counter at the Manhattan shop. If you are interested, however, you may write to Krön Chocolatier, 764 Madison Avenue, New York, New York 10021.

Krum's

If you liked Krön's dark chocolate coatings at $12.50 a pound, you'll love Krum's, at a third the price. The chocolate is superb: rich and well to the bitter side of bittersweet. It is a perfect foil for walnuts, hazelnuts, pecans, or almonds in a collection of nut patties which can only be described as bountiful. Each patty is made of whole or half nuts in caramel and chocolate; I counted eight large, whole almonds in one patty and ten whole hazelnuts in another. Krum's milk chocolate is fragrant, a Swiss-style candy which is used most effectively in a butter "krunch"—butterscotch coated in chocolate dusted with bits of (I think) cashews. It's too sweet for my taste, but a friend who is a krunch fanatic pronounced it perfect.

Krum's, which began around 1901 as a pushcart trundled by Jacob S. Krum through the Lower East Side of New York, today operates a 22,000-square-foot store in the Bronx (which they say is the largest candy store in the country), as well as shops in six other upstate New York cities. An old-timer on the New York candy scene, Krum's candy-makers are proud to have taught many of the "newcomers"—Barracini's, Barton's—and left a definite imprint on the market in such specialties as the nut krunch. Krum's mail orders its candy: the terrific nut patties are approximately $4.19 a pound (plus tax) from J. S. Krum, Inc., 2474 Grand Concourse, Bronx, N.Y. 10458.

Lenotre

Lenôtre's French chocolates are the most expensive candies sold in this country, and the most exclusive. They cost $18 a pound and are available only at the two Marshall Field stores in Chicago.

After an introduction like that, it's painful to have to conclude that the extravagant price has more to do with the cost of basic materials back in France (all natural ingredients, nothing artificial, no preservatives) and air freight (the candy is flown directly to Marshall Field to ensure freshness) than with the actual quality of the product.

True, the creams are superb, silkier than anything else I've tasted, with the possible exception of Cable Car's. Even the caramel—a candy that's usually hard and sticky, or soft and sticky—simply flows, smooth and liquid on the tongue. But the coatings just aren't up to par. They are drier than the ordinary Belgian or American coatings, and they lack the subtle flavoring that makes Godiva, Cable Car, and Corné de la Toison d'Or coatings so distinctive. Finally, in chocolates this expensive one somehow expects to find a high proportion of molded shells, rather than enrobing. Not so here; the majority of the Lenôtre pieces are enrobed.

French chocolates used to be a worldwide symbol of fine chocolates, but today they have all but disappeared from the American market. The reason, not surprisingly, is price, and the case of Lenôtre, the only deluxe French chocolates sold in this country, is a good cxample.

Lenôtre is a well-known French food company, specializing in luxury foods. The company, which was founded in 1957 by a former chef, Gaston Lenôtre, used to have its own specialty store in New York City, just down the street from Bloomingdale's. It closed up shop within a year, however, and a lot of people say it was the prices that did them in. That's confirmed by the candy buyer for one southwestern department store not known for penny-pinching among the clientele: "Even here," he says flatly, "the customers just wouldn't pay that price."

If you want to try Lenôtre, though, you don't really have to spend the $18 to do it. Marshall Field will ship fractions of pounds (at the proper fraction of $18, plus shipping costs). For information, Candy Department, Marshall Field, 111 North State Street, Chicago, Illinois, 60690.

Loft
(For a general description of Loft's candy, see Barracini.)

Loft has been in business for more than a century. The first store was opened in 1860, when the company was founded by

William Loft, the son of an English candy-maker. Its 116-year run makes Loft the nation's oldest candy store (Baker has been in business longer, but never sold through its own retail outlets).

The regional chain, with stores principally in New York, New Jersey, and Connecticut, was partially acquired by the Southland Corporation in 1971 and sold to the B-L Corporation in 1976. Today Loft products are sold alongside Barracini brands in both independent outlets and company-owned stores.

Magic Nut Kitchens

Chocolates aren't the main product line from Magic Nut Kitchens, which, together with Fruit Fair, really specializes in nuts, plus gift packages of dried and fresh fruit. Nevertheless, the chocolates are distinctive in themselves, and the one-pound assortment is a good-looking, varied collection of creams, caramels, nuts, and chocolate-covered dried fruits.

Start with the creams. It must be something in the California air or perhaps the California taste that turns creams made by California companies (see Cable Car) into luscious, extra-silky confections without the slightest hint of sugar particles. Magic Nut Kitchen's creams are super creamy; unfortunately, however, I found them too sweet, and some too strongly flavored. The coffee, in particular, is for true coffee-lovers only—a definite coffee taste, almost espresso strength in flavor, far stronger than any other I've come across. I must say, though, that I specifically exempt the chocolate creams from even this minor criticism. Magic Nut Kitchen's chocolate creams are simply marvelous. There's one with nuts and one with mint flavor, and a thicker one, too buttery to be considered fudge, that has a strong, straight-out rum flavor, and I loved them all.

The caramels are better than average, creamy rather than chewy. There are tart jellies; good, fresh nuts; and an absolute pièce de résistance, a chocolate-coated dried fruit that, I think, is apricot (my hesitation comes from the fact that Magic Nut also coats dried kumquats, and I taste the faint acidy tartness of that fruit here). This last is so good that I would unhesitatingly recommend that you order the Magic Nut Kitchen assortment of chocolate-covered dried fruits—dates, apricots, figs, prunes, kumquats, pineapple, ginger, and orange peel—or maybe the fruit-and-nut assortment instead of the mixed assortment if you are about to try this brand for the first time.

The chocolate coating is pretty good, too: a smooth, wonderfully creamy dark chocolate and a nicely flavored milk chocolate. All candies are enrobed, with a good thick coating that melts quickly in your mouth.

Magic Nut Kitchen candies are made under the direction of the parent company, Meshulam's, Inc., which traces its history back to 1934, when it opened a stall at the famous Farmers Market in Los Angeles.

The business has expanded since then, but is still primarily a family enterprise, with a son, a son-in-law, and some grandchildren tending the copper candy-making kettles. President Eli Meshulam, son of founders Salvador and Allegra Meshulam, explains that the candy is still made in small batches.

It is sold at the Farmers Market and at eighteen company-owned stores in California, as well as in major retail stores in California and Hawaii, with several outlets in the neighboring states of Arizona, Nevada, and New Mexico. Magic Nut Kitchens and Fruit Fair also do a thriving mail-order business, and I can testify personally to its efficiency: when an order of mine went astray, a quick note to the company brought a replacement within days. For a catalog: Magic Nut and Fruit Fair, Kitchen and Shipping Plant, 5978 Bowcroft Street, Los Angeles, California 90016.

Pangburn

Pangburn's chocolates make hash out of the common belief that molded chocolate shells are thicker than enrobed coatings. I know it can't really be true, but I got the definite impression that the Pangburn "ruff-dip" coatings in the famous Ragtime assortment were an inch thick, all the way around. The milk chocolate is blended with honey; it is very sweet, very sticky, and very distinctive.

So distinctive, in fact, that it seems to overwhelm the Pangburn centers. The creams, which are very sweet, are hard to tell apart—I couldn't distinguish the orange from the lemon. Other centers, together with the thick, chewy coatings, seem to duplicate the taste of the most popular candy bars in miniature—caramel and nuts with a chocolate coating. The plain nut centers are good; the Brazil nuts are marvelous, large, fresh, and crunchy. There are also good nut clusters, identified on the listing on the bottom of the box as almonds, but tasting to me something like peanuts.

Pangburn also makes a special combination of duo-dipped chocolates, centers immersed first in dark chocolate and then in the honey-milk chocolate. They are rich and sweet beyond your wildest imagining. Because the chocolate is so rich, you may find yourself ending up licking some off your fingers, and ruing the calories as you munch through this easy-melting, palate-drenching collection.

There is a quaint and faintly old-time look to the orange and gold Pangburn Ragtime box, which recalls the chocolate's history. It was invented around 1914 by H. T. Pangburn, a druggist in Fort Worth, Texas, and C. A. Nicol, a Canadian candy-maker. Their special twist was to blend their chocolate with honey, making it heavy and more viscous than the ordinary chocolate. The name came from Irving Berlin's "Alexander's Ragtime Band," and like the song, Pangburn's Ragtime was an instant hit.

By 1917, having added additional items to his candy line, Pangburn moved his operation to a plant in downtown Fort Worth, where it was to remain for the next fifty-two years.

Pangburn joined Riviana Foods (the company that also owns Hebrew National, Romanoff Caviar, and Carolina Rice) in 1967 and moved into a new plant in 1969. Today the candy is sold in fifty states, although distribution is not always uniform outside the South.

Pepperidge Farm

Like its corporate sister company, Godiva, Pepperidge Farm makes its chocolates without preservatives or artificial ingredients, and recommends that you keep the candy cool and dry to preserve freshness for as long as possible.

The two brands are both made at the same factory in Downingtown, Pennsylvania, but they differ considerably in

taste. And in price. Godiva is pure *luxe,* while Pepperidge Farm candies are well-made and tasty, medium-priced at about $2 for a half-pound box.

The milk-chocolate coating (the candy is enrobed) is particularly distinctive, with a faintly aromatic Swiss taste. The centers are rather sweet, and although it may not be typical of all Pepperidge Farm assortments, there were at least six caramels in the half-pound box I tried.

If you like caramels, though, and want your candy free of additives, this is a good buy, in line with the rest of the Pepperidge Farm product list.

First test-marketed in 1974, Pepperidge Farm chocolates are now widely available. If you can't find them close at hand, you can order them by mail. For information and a catalog, write Pepperidge Farm, Mail Order Company, Inc., Old Post Road, P.O. Box 119, Clinton, Connecticut 06413.

When your order arrives (or when you pick up Pepperidge Farm at your candy store), you'll find one nice touch inside, a note to gladden any consumerist's heart. Any number of candy companies guarantee their candies, promising to replace boxes containing broken chocolates, but Pepperidge Farm's note is signed by the general manager, a real person, not one of those made-up consumer-complaint people. He's real, and he answers his mail—promptly.

Perugina

Americans buy boxed chocolates as snack food. Europeans, on the other hand, buy them as gifts for special occasions, weddings, birthdays, anniversaries, and so forth. As a result, European packaging tends to be extravagant and elaborate, and putting a box of Perugina chocolates next to one from any major American manufacturer is a good way to see the difference for yourself.

In the Perugina box every single chocolate is wrapped in a piece of foil (which varies with the center), and some of them have a second piece of foil wrapped around the first as decoration. The boxes themselves, like those from France, Switzerland, and Belgium, are equally elaborate. Some have reproductions of paintings on the covers, some are simply pretty gold and white. If you prefer, Perugina staff people at the Perugina store on Lexington Avenue in New York City will pack loose chocolates into fine china or ceramic dishes, bowls, and vases (at a slightly higher cost, of course).

As for the chocolates inside the wrappings, they are far more interesting for their fillings than for the molded, slightly dry shells. There is a fine coffee, good and flavorful in a dark-chocolate shell; a mandarin orange jelly in light chocolate; an almond cream; a really super chocolate/coffee cream in milk chocolate.

The fruit creams are all slightly sugary, but the slight sandiness is more than compensated for by the piquancy of the flavors; the banana is particularly good.

In addition to the boxed assortments, Perugina sells its candy by the piece (actually, it's best to buy it by fractions of pounds) for approximately $6.95 a pound. And the company also sells small (four- and five-piece boxes) of chocolate cherries in a semiliquid filling (the cherry is tart, not maraschino), and the famous Baci, milk-chocolate nuggets with a whole hazelnut on top. Both come in the same kind of foil wrappings as the rest of the Perugina line.

Perugina has been making candy since 1907. It incorporated in 1923 under the name Perugina—Cioccolate e Confetture (chocolates and confections), and grew rapidly in the period between the two world wars.

Much of the Perugina factory was destroyed during World War II, but restoration was swift, and during the 1950s and 1960s it once again began a period of rapid growth.

Nevertheless, its sole market remained Italy, and in 1969, in an effort to expand its market, Perugina joined Buitoni in a new corporation, IBP (Industrie Buitoni Perugina s.p.a.). Today Perugina maintains one store in New York City and boutiques in department and specialty stores elsewhere.

Russell Stover

Russell Stover chocolates have a lot in common with those made by Candy Cupboard. Both are good, though not gourmet, candy at a reasonable price (about $3 a pound). Both give you generous pieces, and both have similar strong, recognizable flavors in chocolate and in the centers, too.

Stover's milk chocolate is very good, though at times the enrobing seems a bit waxy. The dark chocolate is just great, mild, clear, and flavorful, the perfect match for Stover's straightforward centers.

The nuts are fresh and large; the coconut—in a milk-chocolate macaroon crunch—is yummy; the vanilla nougat, in dark chocolate, is chewy and flavorful; and the caramels, praise be, are just the right consistency; chewy, yet not so chewy that they stick to your teeth.

About the only criticism I've got is that Stover assortments seem to have more milk-chocolate coatings than dark, but the proportion probably matches the preference for milk chocolate among the general candy-buying population. And Stover does make an all-dark (or all-milk) assortment to suit individual tastes.

Mr. and Mrs. Russell Stover of Denver, Colorado, made their first candy for sale in 1923 in the kitchen of their bungalow home and called it Mrs. Stover's Bungalow Candies.

Mr. Stover got top billing about twenty years later, when the name was changed to Russell Stover Candies, but the Stovers are reputed to have shared equally in the creation of a successful business.

Today the Stover candies—Russell Stover and Mrs. Stover's—are sold in more than 700 department stores, in card and gift shops, in more than 150 company-owned retail stores, and like Whitman's, in thousands of drugstores.

Sarotti

Sarotti chocolates are similar to those made by Elite. They have the same interesting, slightly caramelized flavor and the same sturdy construction, a thick, solid bottom and a precise shape. Sarotti, however, is a real find for anyone who likes authentic bitter orange marmalade: most of its fillings are preserved fruit of one kind or another, with a great sugary but bitter taste that is tantalizing as it slides from one side to the other. One drawback: the half-pound box is not thoroughly sealed in cellophane (there is just a wide band that runs around the middle of the package). As a result, the package is more or less open to the air, and if the chocolates have been standing too long on the shelf, they may have dried out slightly.

Schrafft's

Schrafft's Home Style assortment is straightforward, no-nonsense, 100-percent American chocolates. There are good dark-chocolate and milky light-chocolate coatings, and fillings straight out of an innocent past: thick squares of acid-sweet raspberry jelly; huge fluffy marshmallows in dark chocolate, which taste fantastic if you chill them almost to freezing first; good creams, light and neither too sweet nor cloying.

The pieces are large and absolutely regular in shape, no matter what shape they are. In fact, the only complaint I have about this well-priced, well-made assortment (aside from a definite lack of panache) has to do with my consumerist view. The problem is the packaging: the one-pound box of Home Style is exactly the same size as the two-pound box of chocolates from See's. The See's candies, though, are packed in close together, while the Schrafft's candy is arranged in plastic trays, and none of them are closer than one-quarter to one-half inch. The result is that from the outside the bountiful box looks as though it will offer more candy than it really does.

The price, however, does reflect the poundage, which is clearly stated on the lid, so mine may be only a purist's complaint.

The original Schrafft Candy Company has been defunct for about twenty years. During part of that time, Schrafft candies were manufactured and sold by the Helm Products organization of Boston. In 1974 Schrafft was sold once again, and today the candy is made and sold by Gulf + Western. It is part of the Gulf + Western Consumer Products Group.

See's

See's is a California company, and although there are kitchens in both Los Angeles and San Francisco, the candy is southern California through and through, each piece as big and bouncy as an old-time Hollywood startlet. The taste is southern California, too, creamy and satisfying, with few sophisticated overtones.

This is candy to enjoy without worrying about arcane gourmet standards. The creams are good, smooth, and strong. There's a marvelous maple walnut, a good strong coffee, a malty chocolate in dark or light coating covered with sprinkles, and an interesting, though sugary fruit that may or may not be pineapple.

See's also goes in for the kind of banana-split layering that made Wil Wright's sundaes famous: a whipped marshmallow on top of caramel; marshmallow and nuts; maple cream with nuts and a wee maraschino cherry. All are covered with either mild dark chocolate or mild milk chocolate, neither of which interferes in any way with the terrific mishmash of the fillings.

All in all, at approximately $2.80 a pound this is a great buy for a night of innocent chocolate orgying.

If the innocence of the candy isn't enough to stamp See's as a homey, folksy kind of product, consider this: the whole company—which now numbers nearly two hundred shops in Arizona, California, Colorado, Hawaii, Nevada, Oregon, Texas, Utah, and Washington—was started by a seventy-one-year-old grandmother, Mary See, who opened her first small neighborhood store in 1921.

Fifty years later, See's candies are still made to her recipes and sold only in See's stores so that the company can control freshness by controlling shelf life.

If you live outside the See's territories, not to worry: the company will ship the candy directly to you. For price lists and particulars, write to See's Candies, 3423 South La Cienega Boulevard, Los Angeles, California 90016.

Stuckey's

Stuckey's doesn't make assorted chocolates, and by rights shouldn't really be included in this section. The company is famous for its mastery of the regional candies so dear to the southern sweet tooth—pralines, nougats, nut rolls, and divinity, all sugar-syrup-based confections that stand up to southern climates much better than chocolate does.

Nevertheless, there's no point to a rule that can't be broken, and Stuckey's chocolate pralines and fudge (not to mention their chocolate-covered coconut patties and nuts) are reason enough for me.

The fudge is terrific. Some people like fudge so smooth you can't taste any sugar particles, but I find that kind of fudge tends to stick to the roof of my mouth. Stuckey's fudge isn't exactly Rocky Road, but it does have a slight grittiness, so that you can really taste the chocolate.

As for the pralines, they are simply super. If you've never tasted a praline, it's a flat blob of fudge-like candy (Stuckey makes them in coconut and maple pecan as well as chocolate), drier than fudge and, here at least, slightly smoother. Actually, the Stuckey's pralines reminded me most of the fudge I used to make as a kid—dark, very chocolaty and flat as a pancake, never, for some reason, high enough in the pan to make the kind of regular squares you always saw in magazine ads.

Stuckey's was launched in 1931 by W. S. Stuckey, whose first venture into the food industry was a pecan-buying business. In 1936 Mr. Stuckey opened a roadside stand about five miles out of Eastman, Georgia, where he sold pecans and pecan candy whipped up by Mrs. Stuckey.

Several million pecans later, in 1948 Stuckey began to purchase the machinery for a large-scale candy business and to create the chain of Stuckey shops. There are now more than three hundred of them, coast to coast.

Like Whitman's, Stuckey's is a subsidiary of Pet, Incorporated. Its headquarters, however, are still in Eastman, and its quality hasn't wavered one iota. If there's no Stuckey's store in your town (and you can't find a franchise display in one of the major stores in your area), you can order the candy direct from Stuckey's Stores, P.O. Box 370, Eastman, Georgia 31023.

Terry's of York

There's a definitely English taste to Terry's candy—the dark chocolate is very, very sweet, while the light is bland and milky. (For comparison, try Cadbury's plain milk or dark bars, which have the same general flavors.)

The candy is well-made, some molded, some enrobed, all packed into neat two-tiered, lift-top boxes that have handy guides printed inside the lids, showing exactly what is where inside the box.

The mixture is rather imaginative, with lots of different kinds of centers in both the Devon Milk and All Gold (dark chocolate) assortments. There's a tangerine cream, as well as a honey one, a strawberry, a vanilla, and a walnut. There are chocolate cups; rum truffles, whose flavor is decidedly more chocolate than rum; a custardy lemon filling; a bright green marzipan; and a nice smooth caramel. I got an extra bonus in my box of Devon Milk (or at least one that wasn't listed on the cover), six round pastilles, flat round chocolate candies about the size of a dime.

None of the flavorings is strong enough to obliterate the primary taste, which is chocolate. If your preference is English, Terry's has your taste.

Joseph Terry & Sons, Ltd., is a veritable granddaddy among candy companies. It was founded in York in 1767, during the reign of George III.

Today Terry's is known for its chocolates, but it didn't even get into that end of the business (its first products were sugar candies) until the middle of the nineteenth century, when "eating" chocolates began to replace "drinking" chocolate.

Since then, however, Terry's has made up for lost time. Its first chocolate factory was opened in 1886; the company pioneered the introduction of boxed assortments during the early 1900s, and today Terry's controls about 3 percent of the entire English chocolate market. The company is now part of the Trust Houses Forte Group.

In price, Terry's milk-chocolate assortment compares favorably with American candy ($4 a pound); the dark chocolates are somewhat higher (about $6 a pound).

Tobler

Tobler's chocolates are beautiful. The pieces are large and

glossy, and the quality of the enrobing is so attractive that it rivals even the best molded candy in appearance.

The flavor of the candy is distinctive, a pure Swiss flavor that you will recognize the minute you taste it. The thick milk-chocolate coating (and the solid milk-chocolate pieces) are more aromatic than any other I've tasted; the dark chocolate is mild, sweet, rich, and creamy, typical Swiss conched chocolate.

Because the coatings are so thick and their flavor so predominant, the centers are less imaginative than some other brands'. Nevertheless, they are excellent. There is a good mild chocolate fudge, a coconut with something extra added (fruit? liqueur?), a strong, slightly sugary coffee cream, and a lovely chocolate rum cream. The creams are firm and smooth, rather than liquidy.

Like French chocolates, Swiss chocolates are expensive, owing to the high cost of the basic ingredients. A half-pound of Tobler's chocolates, for example, sells for over $5.

Whitman

The Whitman Sampler is as good as its name. There were no less than thirty-eight different kinds of candy among the forty-five pieces in my one-pound box. And everything from the Pistachio Royale through the Rum Raisin Swirl to the Peanut Butter Puff was clearly listed in the neat, two-layer diagram that appears on the inside of every Sampler box.

Whitman's special distinction among American chocolate-makers is that it makes its own chocolate, right from the bean. The milk chocolate is sweet and rather unprepossessing, but the dark chocolate is typically American, a slightly grainy blend, sweeter than most and reminiscent of Hershey's Special Dark or Maillard's German Sweet bars. The chocolate goes nicely with almost every center, but is especially good on the chocolate cherry cordials, which are also sold separately (Whitman's has a four-piece box of chocolate cherries, too, as well as a miniature, four-piece Sampler).

According to Whitman, the Sampler assortment has barely changed in the past few years. (When the sugar-coated Jordan almonds were removed, so many letters protesting the move were received that they were put back almost immediately.)

At slightly more than $3 a pound, The Sampler (introduced in 1912) is probably the most popular medium-priced candy around, its popularity due not only to quality but to the intelligence of the Whitman decision to market the candy in the "better" drugstores, which attract a more varied audience than any candy store ever could. Today, Whitman, like Stuckey's, is a division of Pet, Incorporated.

The Ultimate Nut

The Ultimate Nut sells a collection of chocolate-covered dried and preserved fruits that are, well, *ultimate*. The chocolate is dark and scrumptious. The orange peel is nicely bitter. The orange slices have a lovely citrus tang. The dried apricots (whole ones, I think) are plump and moist. And the ginger, which usually takes the top of your mouth off (if it doesn't just lie there limp and damp) is a wonder, a sublime blend of pungent fruit in a thicker than normal coating of that yummy chocolate. The raisins are great, and there is one large, clumpy piece, which I think had walnuts and prune in it, that is so darkly sweet and good, I don't even care if I'm wrong. I'm still rummaging through the box for a chocolate-covered kumquat, which should be smashing.

The regular assorted chocolates, alas, are variable. I found the fruit creams just too bland and sweet, and the caramels ordinary. But even a confirmed Easterner like me could forgive California anything—freeways, smog, Richard Nixon—for a guaranteed supply of the rum-chocolate truffle covered with dark chocolate and topped with sprinkles. Not to mention the plain chocolate fudge, or the coconut covered in dark chocolate, a moist and luscious grown-up version of the Mounds bars I loved as a child.

Pick up Ultimate Nut candies at the Farmers Market in LA, or the Studio City store, or order through the catalogue from The Ultimate Nut, 11849 Ventura Boulevard, Studio City, California 91604.

6: HOT CHOCOLATE, COCOA, AND CORDIALS

A steaming cup of dark and aromatic chocolate or a paler one of sweetened cocoa is one of nature's noble drinks, on a par with a fine malt Scotch, a grand champagne, or your very own blend of individually ground coffee.

If you find it hard to square that with the taste of the sweetish, milky glop you get at the corner candy store, it may be because what you are drinking is sweetish, milky glop and not hot chocolate after all.

At the start, of course, all chocolate was served in liquid form, and if the legends are even half true, it was a pretty potent drink. Time and the rigors of industrial cultivation have lowered the potency by weeding out the strongest, quasi-intoxicating beans, and our tastes have changed, too, so that the cold, bitter, peppery drink that Montezuma served is not the sort of thing we'd want today.

You might find the version served in the seventeenth and the eighteenth century slightly more palatable, and if you could beg, borrow, or steal a handful of beans (it won't be easy today, when cocoa beans are sold only in forty-ton truck-loads), this is how they made it:*

700 cocoa beans
1–1½ lbs. sugar
2 oz. cinnamon
14 peppercorns from Mexico
½ oz. cloves
3 vanilla beans, or, instead, 2 ounces
  of aniseed
the biggest part of a hazelnut

* Recipe courtesy of the Nestlé Company.

You really should roast the beans first, to make it easier to get the shells off. The idea, then, is to mash everything together with mortar and pestle (being careful to fish out any shells you've missed), and then to add hot water and whip the whole thing to a froth. "Some people," the recipe explains, "add a small amount of orange-flower water, a grain of musc (sic), or ambergris. . . . Others omit the clove, musc, ambergris and orange-flower water, but add almonds, hazelnuts and powder of roses from Alexandria."

Of course, there's an easier way.

If you're willing to be a bit discriminating when you shop, ruthlessly weeding out the kids' cocoa mixes and searching for real drinking chocolate, you can enjoy a sophisticated, lovingly brewed cup of hot chocolate or cocoa, rich with the flavors you've been missing.

Hot Chocolate

To make a potent hot chocolate, you have to start with an authentic drinking chocolate—a chocolate liquor to which sugar and any one or two or three of a number of spices such as vanilla, cinnamon, and nutmeg have been added.

This kind of chocolate is usually sold in hardened bar or tablet form, with directions for melting printed handily on the package. If you try to nibble on the bar, however, as you might on any ordinary chocolate bar, you will find a number of obvious differences between the two.

To begin with, there is the matter of richness, or the fat content. All eating chocolate is chocolate liquor *plus* additional cocoa butter to make it richer, softer, and more meltable. Drinking chocolate usually doesn't have any extra cocoa butter added, since that would only melt down into a greasy layer of oil on top of the cup. As a result if you bite into a bar of drinking chocolate, it will fight back a bit. It's hard, and it won't melt quickly or smoothly in your mouth.

Because of the necessary variation in cocoa-butter content, most eating chocolate bars can't be used for hot chocolate. There are, however, a few surprising exceptions: Maillard's, for example, isn't bad (although it could use some milk powder mixed in to soak up some of the richness of the chocolate) and Baker's Unsweetened squares melt down fairly well in hot chocolate as long as you use the blender method (see below) to make the drink.

You'll also find a big difference in texture between chocolate meant for eating and that meant for melting. The sugar in the eating chocolate has been smoothed down exceedingly fine so that there are no rough edges, or almost none, to irritate your tongue. The sugar in bars of drinking chocolate, however, is rough and scratchy. The reason is simple economics, as well as practical cookery: why waste time and money smoothing down sugar particles that are going to dissolve anyway the minute they hit the hot water?

As for taste, bars of drinking chocolate are apt to be more highly flavored than regular chocolate bars, and again the reason is quite simple: diluted in hot water, the strong spicing will smooth out to a more subtle flavor.

Despite the differences in texture, richness, and taste, there are people who enjoy nothing more than chomping away on a gritty, sweet, lumpy, spicy bar of drinking chocolate.

If you'd like to give it a try—or to make a distinctive, authoritative hot chocolate—you should know that most of the drinking chocolate sold in this country is made in Latin America, actually Mexico and Puerto Rico. The Latin American countries have a long history of romance with drinking chocolates, of course. The first chocolate, served as a liquid, was discovered in Mexico, and probably the climate, hot and sticky, made low-fat chocolates a far more practical way of keeping chocolate—far more practical, for example, than trying to keep fine boxed chocolates, with their high cocoa-butter content and their intricately made centers, from melting in the Latin American sun.

You can find bars of drinking chocolate in any Latin American *bodega* and even in a growing number of strictly Anglo grocery stores that, having noted an increasing consumer call for ethnic foods, now stock them, too, right alongside the refried beans.

If you can find them in your town, the following brands

will give you an idea of the taste and variety of authentic hot chocolate.

Cortés. This is an eight-ounce bar, divided into one-ounce strips. The chocolate is quite light in color and light in taste as well. It is very sweet, even when melted into hot water, and is not terribly spicy. Cortés chocolate is made by the Cortés Company in Puerto Rico and distributed on the mainland by Goya Foods, which is well-known for its other Spanish foods.

Ibarra. Ibarra chocolate comes packed six round tablets (3.3 ounces each) to a nifty red and yellow cardboard canister. Ibarra is Mexican chocolate, sugary and light in flavor. It is also spicy, loaded with cinnamon, and flavored with almonds. Ibarra is heavily sugared and much lighter on the tongue than any of the other drinking chocolates. It melts more quickly, too, rather like cotton candy, ephemeral and sweet. Ibarra is made by Chocolatera de Jalisco in Guadalajara and sold in California and, by some quirk of distribution, in Chicago.

Goya. Goya sells a dark, chocolaty bar, a rectangle divided into eight one-ounce strips that are nicely scored across the middle so that you can break them into half-ounce tablets. The chocolate, which is made in Puerto Rico, is rich and very good, the only one, in fact, which tasted right (as an eating chocolate) when I tried it straight out of the wrapper. It makes superb hot chocolate, slightly sweeter than Menier. (The bar is distributed by Goya Foods.)

Menier. Menier, like Cortés, is an eight-ounce bar divided into one-ounce strips. The chocolate, however, is richer then Cortés, darker and less sweet. Originally a French product (with the medals on the wrapper to prove its merit), Menier is now manufactured in Puerto Rico and can be found in Latin American groceries as well as some gourmet markets. This is the most bittersweet of the drinking chocolates.

HOW TO MAKE HOT CHOCOLATE

Because I like my chocolate more or less thin and straight, my test for any hot chocolate is to (1) break one ounce of chocolate into small pieces, (2) put the pieces in a tall, thin cup and just cover with boiling water, (3) mash to a paste, (4) add more water—about 4½ ounces—and whip with a long-tined fork or wisk. This makes a light, interesting drink if the chocolate is strong enough, and you can enliven it with a dash of pepper or cinnamon if there isn't any seasoning in the chocolate to begin with.

I find that this simple method works best with the Menier chocolate, which is stronger than Cortés, more chocolaty than Ibarra, and less sweet than Goya.

You can make any of these richer by adding a teaspoon or two of powdered* or condensed milk. Blend it thoroughly into the mashed chocolate before you add the rest of the hot water, and stir vigorously to be certain that the entire drink is mixed well.

Powdered milk gives you a lighter and less fattening drink than condensed milk, but you may prefer the richer version. I prefer both of these to fresh milk. Using them gives you better control over the texture of the drink, and frankly I find them more economical and dependable, for you can store them both without having to worry about their going bad while still unopened on the shelf.

Hot chocolate also goes well with coffee. Café Louvois, a European favorite, is made with equal parts of hot chocolate and hot black coffee topped with whipped cream. Café Muck, on the other hand, is hot espresso with a dash of kirsch and a piece of chocolate dropped in. The topping, of course, is whipped cream.

I've used the word "dissolve" a few times to explain what happens with chocolate and hot water, but the scientific fact is that chocolate does not dissolve, it disperses. That means that the tiny particles of chocolate float in the liquid and that,

* In powder form, not mixed with liquid.

if you make your hot chocolate in the simple way described above, you may be able to taste the grittiness in your drink.

You can avoid that by using an electric blender. The blender will aeratc the liquid and fluff it up so that it tastes smoother and richer, and at the same time will disperse the chocolate particles more thoroughly. It will also evenly distribute any fat particles in the chocolate, so that you can use a very rich chocolate without having to contend with a thick layer of oil on top of the drink, as you would have if you simply melted the fattier chocolate in water.

Maillard's chocolate bar can be used for hot chocolate prepared in a blender and so can Baker's Unsweetened squares. I make no promises, though, for any other bar chocolate, although there's no reason at all why you can't experiment on your own.

In doing so, you will find that the chocolates with higher fat content probably taste better with powdered milk, since the condensed milk, which is rich itself, may make them too heavy.

BASIC RECIPES FOR HOT CHOCOLATE—AND SOME VARIATIONS

Use the blender method to prepare each of the following variations on a perfectly delicious theme. Each will give you one full eight-ounce cup.

1 oz. Cortés, Goya, or Menier chocolate
½-1 oz. liqueur (to taste)
5 oz. boiling water

Break chocolate into pieces and blend all ingredients until frothy. You may use any of the following liqueurs: Amaretto (almond liqueur), white crème de menthe, any absolutely plain fruit liqueur (orange, any of the berries), any plain chocolate (Arrow's crème de cacao is quite good) to make the drink even more chocolaty and potent, or a peppermint liqueur (plain, please, with no other flavoring).

Do not use Ibarra chocolate as a base when you plan to add any fruit liqueur, peppermint, or crème de menthe; the cinnamon flavoring in the chocolate will simply overwhelm any other flavoring.

2 sections of an Ibarra tablet
(3 tsp. fat-free powdered milk; optional)
dash pepper
5 oz. boiling water

Blend to a froth. The pepper gives the chocolate a fascinating taste, perhaps much like that enjoyed by Mexican and Spanish ladies in the sixteenth and seventeenth centuries.

1 oz. Baker's Unsweetened Chocolate
2 tsp. sugar (or less, depending on taste)
(2 tsp. dry milk; optional)
(½ jigger Amaretto; optional)
5 oz. boiling water

Blend to a froth. Baker's chocolate is much richer than any of the three drinking chocolates, and you may prefer one to the other. You can make the chocolate almost unbearably rich by using condensed milk. Adding Amaretto to the mixture is an incredibly sensual experience. (NOTE: You can also use Maillard's chocolate in this recipe, but if you do, be sure to leave out the sugar.)

Serve your hot chocolate in tall, skinny cups, which keep the heat in and let the aroma out. You can use a cinnamon stick garnish or a piece of orange peel, fresh or preserved, with any chocolate except Ibarra.

Cocoa

To make a truly splendid cup of hot cocoa, you have to start with good cocoa, and absolutely nothing else. That means tossing out all the instant, quick, make-it-in-the-cup mixtures you've accumulated and starting from scratch with (1) cocoa powder, (2) sugar, (3) milk, (4) water, and (5) whatever seasonings you prefer.

It may take a little extra time, but the difference in taste will be worth it and so will the difference in price. Ounce for ounce, plain cocoa costs considerably less than cocoa-plus-everything, and one ounce of cocoa will go much further than one ounce of any of the mixes.

As far as I know, there is only one brand of absolutely plain cocoa powder available nationally, Hershey's. There are two brands of cocoa with only vanilla added, Droste and Van Houten. (Both of these are Dutched cocoas.) Although the selection is limited, even these three will give you a nice variety of tastes that can be further varied according to the other ingredients you add.

Droste. I might have had some reservations about Droste's chocolate bars, but I have none at all about the Droste cocoa, which is marvelous—mild, flavorful, and pleasant. The recipe on the Droste box calls for a 1:1 ratio of cocoa and sugar, but I find it works better this way:

2 heaping tsp. Droste cocoa
1½–2 level tsp. sugar
2 level tsp. powdered (or condensed) milk
5 oz. boiling water

> Mix all the dry ingredients (and condensed milk) in a large mug. Add a bit of hot water and blend to a paste, then add the rest of the hot water, mixing vigorously. Makes an eight-ounce serving.

Hershey. Hershey's cocoa is extraordinarily low in fat, 14–15 percent as compared to Van Houten's 25 percent (the FDA requires that breakfast cocoas have at least 22 percent cocoa butter). Because it is not Dutched cocoa, Hershey's has a somewhat harsher taste than Droste or Van Houten. People who like Hershey's dark-chocolate bars, however, will like the Hershey cocoa, which has the added advantage of being totally free of all flavoring. I find Hershey works best if the sugar is precisely equal to the cocoa.

2 tsp. Hershey cocoa
2 tsp. sugar
½ tsp. vanilla extract (another flavoring, such as peppermint or orange, may be substituted or used in combination with the vanilla, ¼ tsp. each)
3–4 tsp. powdered milk (or 2–3 tsp. condensed)
5 oz. very hot water

Combine all dry ingredients (and condensed milk) in a large mug. Add the flavoring and a bit of water, and blend everything to a very smooth paste. Add the rest of the water and mix vigorously.

Because Hershey's cocoa is so low in fat, it may (with your doctor's permission) be acceptable for people who are on a controlled-fat, low-cholesterol diet and can't use regular forms of chocolate.

Van Houten. One expects the taste of Van Houten cocoa to be the truest sample of a Dutched cocoa flavor. That flavor seems to me to be slightly harsher than Droste (although measurably milder than Hershey's) and somewhat similar to the taste of Van Houten chocolate bars.

The cocoa comes in a nice reusable tin, and the directions on the label say to mix it at a ratio of one teaspoon cocoa to two teaspoons sugar. I find that a bit sweet and prefer the following recipe instead:

1 tsp. Van Houten cocoa
1½ tsp. sugar
1 tsp. condensed milk
5 oz. boiling water

As with all the other recipes listed here, mix the dry ingredients, then add the condensed milk, the boiling water, and whip to a froth in a large mug.

Of course, you can use a variety of spices in your hot cocoa—nutmeg, cinnamon, allspice (powdered), pepper, and mint.

Because cocoa is lighter than hot chocolate and the particles disperse more easily in hot water, all the recipes here may be mixed right in the cup. However, you can also blend your cocoas to produce an exceedingly light and foamy drink. Or you may cook them directly in the pot, substituting fresh whole milk or a mixture of milk and cream for the liquids and condensed or powdered milk I've listed. If you choose to do so, heat the liquids, *but do not allow them to boil.* Then add cocoa and other ingredients and cook gently for a minute or so and pour into heated mugs or cups. (If you use hot chocolate rather than cocoa, reverse the process: melt the chocolate in the top of a double boiler, then add hot or scalded milk, cook a minute, and whip until smooth and frothy.) For the richest possible drink, beat in an egg yolk.

Cordials

In the very best cordials (or liqueurs; the terms are interchangeable) the chocolate taste comes from flavorings distilled directly from the cocoa nibs. Like other extracts, these flavorings can be colorless, which is why crème de cacao can be clear, instead of brown.

The possibilities for embellishing on chocolate liqueurs are endless. There are plain chocolates, plus chocolates with mint, with coconut, with fruit. How good they are may depend upon how much they cost. In other forms of chocolate, price may be irrelevant to taste, but in chocolate cordials it seems to correlate—the more expensive brands, quite simply, taste better. If they are combinations, their flavors are truer and more distinct.

The following is a sampler to give you a taste of the various kinds of chocolate liqueurs:

Crème de cacao
- Arrow (clear)
- DuBouchett (dark)

Mint-flavored
Vandermint (chocolate mint)

Coconut
Choclair

Fruit
Cheri-Suisse (cherry)
Leroux Chocolate Banana
Sabra (orange-chocolate)

Chocolate Candy
Marmot (bits of chocolate floating in liqueur)

Any one of these liqueurs, or any other liqueur you prefer, will taste especially good if you serve it in a tiny cup made of bittersweet chocolate. The cups are made by the Astor Chocolate Corporation, and if you cannot find them in your area, you can order them from Astor, 48-25 Metropolitan Avenue, Brooklyn, New York 11237. They come packed twelve to a box, and the minimum order is three boxes at a total cost of about $7.50. (Astor also makes chocolate dessert shells, sold six to a box, with a minimum order of three boxes for $8.25.)

Chocolate cocktails. The classic chocolate cocktail, of course, is the Brandy Alexander, equal parts (usually 3/4 oz.) brandy, crème de cacao, and cream shaken with ice and strained into a chilled cocktail glass. You may vary this recipe by using any of the flavored chocolate cordials (with fruit, mint, or coconut) and substituting gin for the brandy.

All the cordials go nicely with ice cubes and club soda as spritzers in tall, frosted glasses, and all are fine straight, in cordial glasses, or on the rocks.

If you'd like something more complex, try one of these:

Chocolate Mint Julep

Pour one ounce of chocolate mint liqueur over crushed ice in a tall glass. Add an ounce and a half of bourbon, stir, then add a last dash of liqueur to the top of the drink. Garnish with fresh mint.

Chocolate Screwdriver

Half-fill a tall glass with ice cubes. Pour in one-half ounce of orange-chocolate liqueur, add an ounce of vodka, and fill the glass with orange juice (about four–five ounces). Stir.

Rum Chocolate

Crème de cacao and rum are natural allies. Pour one ounce of pale rum, one-half ounce each of crème de cacao and crème de menthe (or one ounce of chocolate-mint liqueur) into a cocktail shaker partially filled with cracked ice. Add one-half ounce of cream and just the slightest dash of very dark rum. Shake well, strain into a cocktail glass (prechilled), and add one last dash of dark rum on top.

7: CLASSIC CHOCOLATE COOKING

Chocolate Cake

Before the invention of cocoa, chocolate-lovers used to cut the fattiness of drinking chocolate by combining it with some form of starch. (When the starch was added without the purchaser's knowledge, to stretch the chocolate and later the cocoa, it was regarded as an adulterant.)

This mixture of chocolate with starches and flours—rice, wheat, or corn—was a natural alliance that eventually produced the chocolate cake.

Chocolate Cake

1 3/4 cups sifted cake flour
1 tsp. cream of tartar
3/4 tsp. baking soda
1 tsp. salt
½ cup shortening*
1½ cups sugar
2 eggs
Milk*
3 squares unsweetened chocolate, melted
1 tsp. vanilla

Sift flour with cream of tartar, baking soda, and salt. Cream shortening; gradually beat in sugar. Add eggs, one at a time, beating well after each egg is added. Add flour alternately with milk, a small amount at a time, beating after each addition until smooth. Blend in chocolate and vanilla.

Divide batter between two 9-inch layer pans that have

* With vegetable shortening, use 1 cup plus 2 tbsp. milk. With butter or margarine, use 1 cup milk.

been lined on the bottom with paper. Bake at 350°F. for 30 to 35 minutes or until cake tester comes out clean. Cool in pans for 10 minutes; then remove from pans, remove paper, and cool on racks.

(Alternate baking pans: three 9-inch layer pans at 375°F. for 20 minutes; one 13x9-inch pan at 350°F. for 45 to 50 minutes.)

*Hungarian Chocolate Frosting**

- 6 squares (6-oz.) semi-sweet chocolate, such as Baker's
- 1 cup sifted confectioner's sugar
- 2 tbsp. hot water
- Dash of salt
- 2 egg yolks
- ¼ cup butter or margarine, at room temperature

Partially melt chocolate over very low heat. Remove from heat, stir rapidly until entirely melted. Add sugar, water, and salt; blend thoroughly. Add egg yolks, one at a time, beating well after each. Add butter, 1 Tbs. at a time, beating thoroughly after each addition. Makes 1½ cups.

Chocolate Fondues

The fondue is a national pastime in Switzerland. Put that together with the fact that the Swiss eat more chocolate per capita than any other country in the world, and you can easily see how the chocolate fondue was born.

Fondue Toblerone

(AS SERVED AT THE SWISS CENTER RESTAURANT IN NEW YORK)

* Recipe reproduced with the permission of Walter Baker Chocolates, General Foods Corporation.

3 3-oz. bars of Toblerone Milk Chocolate
½ cup light or heavy cream
2 tbsp. brandy or rum
Assorted dunkables

Break chocolate into an earthenware fondue pot or a small chafing dish. Add cream and brandy. Stir over low heat until chocolate is melted and mixture is smooth. Serve over candle warmer or very low flame.

The honey nougat in the Toblerone chocolate seems to give the fondue an extra, creamy richness. If you like a dark chocolate, by all means use Toblerone's bittersweet. People who prefer a nonalcoholic dish might try one tablespoon of instant coffee in place of the brandy.

The dunkables can include any kind of cake—ladyfingers, macaroons, and pieces of pound cake. On a warm summer's evening, fresh fruit—chunks of apple, pineapple, oranges, and bananas—are particularly good. So are whole strawberries, which are luscious with the following fondue.

Chocolate Mint Fondue *

6 oz. semisweet chocolate pieces (either baking chips or your favorite bar, broken up)
1 cup sour cream
½ cup chocolate-mint liqueur, such as Vandermint

Melt chocolate pieces in fondue pot or chafing dish. Stir in sour cream and chocolate-mint liqueur. Serve warm.

Chocolate Mousses

There is no mistaking the French ancestry of *mousse au chocolat*, which was invented by Henri de Toulouse-Lautrec, the artist who brought to his cooking the same inventive zest he brought to his paintings of the Parisian demimondaines.

*Adapted from a recipe created by Joseph E. Seagram & Sons, Inc.

Toulouse-Lautrec called his invention *chocolate mayonnaise;* in Switzerland the same general recipe is often referred to as chocolate parfait, which in America means ice cream.

Orange Chocolate Cream Mousse *

4 ounces semisweet chocolate
¼ cup orange or orange-chocolate liqueur, such as Sabra
4 egg whites
⅛ tsp. salt
⅛ tsp. cream of tartar
2 tbsp. sugar
4 egg yolks
½ cup heavy whipping crean

Melt chocolate over hot water. Cool. Stir in liqueur. Beat egg whites with salt, cream of tartar, and sugar until stiff. Beat egg yolks until thick; stir into chocolate. Whip cream and fold into chocolate with beaten egg whites. Spoon into parfait dishes and chill. Makes 6–8 servings.

Mocha Mousse †

4 tbsp. dark crème de cacao, such as DuBouchett
4 tbsp. coffee brandy
2 tbsp. water
⅔ cup sugar
Pinch of salt
1 egg, beaten
2 tbsp. sifted confectioners' sugar
1 pt. heavy whipped cream, stiffly whipped

Cook 3 tbsp. each crème de cacao and coffee brandy, with next 3 ingredients until syrup will spin a thread (230° F.). Slowly add syrup and remaining liqueur to beaten egg, beating constantly. Cook in double boiler, stirring constantly, about 5 minutes, or until thickened. Cool mixture, then refrigerate until cold. Blend well and fold liqueur mixture and confectioners' sugar into whipped cream. Put mixture in fancy 1-qt. mold and freeze.

* Adapted from a recipe prepared by Joseph E. Seagram & Sons, Inc.
† Reprinted by permission of DuBouchett cordials.

Low-fat Chocolate Yogurt Mousse

1 8-oz. cup vanilla yogurt
4 oz. Hershey's cocoa
4 oz. sugar

Blend all the ingredients gently by hand, to smooth out the cocoa lumps. *Do not whip the mixture or use an electric blender as this will liquefy the yogurt.* Pour into a chilled bowl and store in the refrigerator for several hours. The resulting mousse should be thick and stiff, although I would not guarantee its holding its shape in a mold. Should you like a more acid taste, you might try plain yogurt instead of vanilla.

Chocolate Pudding

If your idea of a chocolate pudding is what you make from a packaged mix, then the following recipe should open your eyes to the delights of a sophisticated pudding meant strictly for gourmet eating.

Chocolate Floating Islands
(AS SERVED AT LA MANGEOIRE RESTAURANT IN NEW YORK)

1 oz. Grand Marnier liqueur
1 tsp. vanilla
1½ pt. milk
Lemon zest (of ¼ lemon)
12 egg yolks
1¼ lb. sugar
5½ oz. bitter chocolate
12 egg whites
Pinch of salt
Juice of ½ lemon

Preparation of the cream base

Boil the milk with the lemon zest. Add egg yolks to ¾ lb. sugar in a large bowl and mix well, then add boiled milk. Once the mixture has been well blended, pour it back into the pot in which the milk was boiled. Heat slowly over a low flame until this mixture thickens, but do not allow it to boil. Add Grand Marnier and vanilla.

Melt the chocolate and add. Mix well and pour into a deep dessert bowl. Refrigerate.

Preparation of the "islands" (once the cream has been chilled)

Beat the egg whites slowly while adding a pinch of salt and the juice of ½ lemon. Once the lemon juice has been added, beat the egg whites at high speed until they are firm, but not granulated. Add ¼ lb. sugar and beat for another three minutes. Poach small mounds of meringue (islands) in hot water for about ten minutes, then place cooked "islands" on top of the chilled cream, and decorate with shaved chocolate.

Chocolate Sauces

Like most other elaborate chocolate cookery, chocolate sauce is a nineteenth-century creation. Chocolate sauce over specially spiced pears is called Poire Belle Hélène, a favorite of French cuisine and of the great French chef Escoffier.

Hot chocolate sauce #1 *

7 oz. bitter chocolate
3 oz. sugar
1½ oz. butter
4 egg yolks

Over a low heat, mix together the chocolate, sugar, and butter. Melt and boil up briefly. Remove from heat and quickly beat in the egg yolks. The sauce must be kept hot but must not be boiled again. Pour immediately over spiced pears.

Pears for Poire Belle Hélène

Marinate pear halves from large can (1 lb. 13 oz.) in juice from can, flavored with a dash of cognac, a dash of mara-

* Adapted from a recipe published by Chocosuisse, the Union of Swiss Chocolate Manufacturers, and reprinted with their permission.

schino, and a teaspoon of vanilla sugar [made by putting a whole vanilla bean in a jar with 1 lb. sugar and leaving overnight or for 48 hours].

Serve pear halves on ice cream or on a piece of pound cake, topped with Hot Chocolate Sauce #1.

Hot Chocolate Sauce #2 *

1 cup semisweet chocolate pieces
1 tbsp. butter
1 tbsp. light corn syrup
¼ cup light cream
¼ cup chocolate-mint liqueur (such as Vandermint)

Melt chocolate and butter together. Remove from heat. Stir in corn syrup, cream, and liqueur. Pour over ice cream, or pear halves marinated in ½ cup liqueur for one hour.

Chocolate syrup is a thinner confection than chocolate sauce, though both will thicken when poured over very cold foods such as ice cream. The following recipe comes from a booklet produced by the Baker company about the turn of the century.

Chocolate Syrup †

⅓ cup breakfast cocoa
2 cups sugar
1 cup boiling water
½ tsp. vanilla (vanillin may be substituted)

Mix cocoa and sugar, add water gradually, and stir constantly until mixture is melted. Then boil five minutes. Cool, and add vanilla (or vanillin).

* Reprinted by permission of Joseph E. Seagram & Sons, Inc.

† Recipe reproduced with the permission of Baker Chocolates, General Foods Corporation.

Chicken Mole

According to legend, the Mole sauce was created by nuns in a convent in the Mexican city of Puebla. The dish, to be served to the visiting bishop for Sunday dinner, was originally made with turkey, a native bird. The peppery sauce was conventionally Mexican, but at the last minute the cooks grated in some bitter chocolate. Though the taste is not exactly chocolate, it is distinctive, and the Mole (whether on turkey or chicken) deserves a place in every chocolate cookbook.

Chicken Mole

(AS SERVED AT THE FONDA LOS MILAGROS IN NEW YORK)

½ lb. *mulato* peppers (green peppers)
¼ lb. *pasilla* peppers (medium-hot red peppers)
3 pieces *chipotle* peppers (very hot red peppers)
2 broilers, cut up into eight pieces
1 clove garlic
1 small onion
¼ lb. tomatoes
8 peppercorns
½ stick cinnamon
1 tsp. cumin
1 small banana
1 piece toasted white bread
1 tortilla (well cooked)
2 oz. raisins
2 oz. almonds
1 oz. peanuts (shelled)
1 oz. plain crackers, crumbled
1 qt. chicken broth
2 squares bitter (baking) chocolate

Cut peppers in half and remove seeds and membranes. Toast in frying pan. In a second frying pan, which has been heated, sauté chicken pieces in vegetable oil (corn oil is suggested). When chicken is browned, remove and reserve. Into hot oil, place garlic (chopped). When it is browned, add the onion (chopped), the tomatoes (cut in wedges), the spices, the banana, the toast, tortilla and crumbled crackers, and the raisins and nuts. When fried a bit, add the peppers. Then remove all ingredients and grind or blend into a paste, adding chicken broth to thin, as required. Place chicken in serving casserole, cover with sauce (adding chicken broth, if needed), and grate in the bitter chocolate. Taste, and correct seasonings, then warm before serving. Serves 8–10.

SOURCES AND FURTHER READING

1. *General information about chocolate and chocolate-making*

The Chocolate Manufacturers Association (CMA) in Washington publishes a short pamphlet called *The Story of Chocolate,* which is about as basic as you can get. It includes a good color chart showing the harvest seasons in major chocolate-producing countries. (The CMA also has two films about chocolate that can be useful for group audiences.) Chocosuisse, the Union of Swiss Chocolate Manufacturers, publishes a more sophisticated booklet called *Chocologie,* which is beautifully illustrated. It contains a lot of historical bits and pieces, as well as biographies of the major Swiss chocolate pioneers and a handful of super recipes. The pamphlet is available in English. *Cocoa,* a booklet published by Merrill, Lynch, Pierce, Fenner and Smith (1966), is out of print now, but much of the material in it, specifically the description of the New York Cocoa Exchange and cocoa trading in New York, is available through the firm's Commodities Department.

There are more detailed articles on chocolate in the *Encyclopaedia Britannica* and the *Larousse Gastronomique* (Crown Publishers, 1961), but the latest and most detailed book about chocolate is *Chocolate Production and Use* by L. Russell Cook (Books for Industry, 1972). This is the bible of the chocolate industry, interesting for the layman who wants to know more about the science and technology of chocolate and chocolate-making. The book is written in basic, clearly understandable terms.

2. *Early contemporary accounts*

Of all the early accounts of chocolate, only Brillat-Savarin's

The Physiology of Taste (Dover Books, 1960) is easily found outside of a research library. Brillat-Savarin wrote his book in 1825, and it includes a lovely chapter on chocolate (meaning hot chocolate) in eighteenth- and early-nineteenth-century France.

All the following are to be located only in libraries, but they are well worth digging up, for they can give you an invaluable look at contemporary mores and manners.

Thomas Gage's *A New Survey of the West Indies* (London, 1648) tells about the first discoveries of cocoa and chocolate in the New World. *Cocoa—All About It,* by Historicus [Richard Cadbury] and *The Food of the Gods,* by Brandon Head, were published within a decade of each other, in 1896 and 1903, in London. Their special emphasis is on the almost magical medical properties of chocolate in Victorian England, and as a bonus, there is the description of the Cadbury chocolate factory at Bournville.

In the United States, the Walter Baker Company of Dorchester, Massachusetts (now a subsidiary of General Foods), published a number of booklets and pamphlets during the late 1890s and early 1900s. The booklets, which have titles such as *Cocoa and Chocolate* and *The Chocolate-Plant and Its Products,* are also to be found only in libraries.

3. *Nutrition*

Aside from the legends and the myths, perhaps the earliest attempt at classifying the nutritional information about cocoa and chocolate is a booklet called the *Bibliography of the Nutritive Value of Chocolate and Cocoa,* which was published by the Hershey Chocolate Company about 1910. Although some of the studies and surveys reported in this bibliography have fallen to more recent knowledge, the scientific attempt is laudable and fascinating.

In modern times the United States government has become a veritable treasure trove of information about chocolate. The Food and Drug Administration publishes standards of identity for all chocolate and cocoa products, and the Department of Agriculture's Handbook No. 8 lists the nutritional content of all kinds of chocolate (as well as for several thousand other foods).

For laymen who need a guide to get through the maze of nutritional terminology, there are three handy paperback guides, written in intelligent and understandable language: *The Natural Foods and Nutrition Handbook,* by Rafael Macia (Perennial Library, 1972); *Eater's Digest,* by Michael F. Jacobson (Anchor, 1972); and *Dictionary of Health and Nutrition,* by Larry Douris and Mark Timon (Pyramid, 1976).

4. *Statistical information*

Gill and Duffus, Ltd., a major cocoa trader, publishes an extremely useful booklet, *Cocoa Statistics* (London, 1970), which contains tables showing the various figures for worldwide cocoa production and distribution. The New York Cocoa Exchange is also a source for statistical information, as is the Department of Commerce, which publishes a booklet called, *Confectionery Manufacturers' Sales and Distribution.*

In Great Britain, the Cocoa, Chocolate and Confectionery Alliance publishes an annual report showing production and sales, and data for other foreign countries is usually available through trade and commerce offices here in the United States, although some countries—notably the United Kingdom, Switzerland, the Netherlands, and Israel—make their information more readily available than others.

5. *Information about individual companies*

In the United States, Hershey and Nestlé maintain the most elaborate consumer-service departments, and a number of chocolate companies such as Baker, which are part of larger corporations, do, too. In England, Cadbury and Joseph Terry & Sons work much the same way, as does Côte d'Or in Belgium (although its material is in French) and Holland's Droste.

Almost all the other chocolate companies are accommodating and pleasant in answering your queries and most will send out recipe brochures upon request (Suchard's and Tobler's are particularly attractive). In all my research, I found only one major company that simply would not answer any of its mail.

DIRECTORY OF CHOCOLATE COMPANIES

Astor Chocolate Company, 48-25 Metropolitan Avenue, Brooklyn, New York 11237

Baker Chocolates, A Division of General Foods, 250 North Street, White Plains, New York 10625

Barracini, The Southland Corporation, 2828 North Haskell Avenue, Dallas, Texas 75204

Barth's, 270 West Merrick Road, Valley Stream, New York 11580

Barton's, Bonbonierre, 80 De Kalb Avenue, Brooklyn, New York 11201

Blum's of San Francisco, 111 North 56th Street, Lincoln, Nebraska 68510

Brigham's, 30 Mill Street, Arlington, Massachusetts 02174

Cable Car Candy Company, 700 West Pacific Coast Highway, Long Beach, California 90806

Cadbury Corporation, Schweppes House, 1200 High Ridge Road, Stamford, Connecticut 06905 (or Cadbury-Schweppes Ltd., 1/10 Connaught Place, London W2 2EX England)

Candy Cupboard, New England Confectionery Company, 254 Massachusetts Avenue, Cambridge, Massachusetts 02319

Cella's Confections, Inc., 327 West Broadway, New York, New York 10013

The Chunky Corporation, The Ward Candy Company, Margaret and James Streets, Philadelphia, Pennsylvania 19137

Chymos, c/o Finn Foods, 135 County Road, Cresskill, New Jersey 07626

Corné de la Toison d'Or, Rue Auguste Lambiotte 79/81, B-1030 Brussels, Belgium

Sucesores Pedro Cortés, GPO Box 3626, San Juan, Puerto Rico 00936

Côte d'Or, Rue Bara 40, B-1070 Brussels, Belgium

Droste Fabrieken B.V., Harmenjansweg 129, P.O.B. 9, Haarlem, Holland

Elite Israel Chocolate & Sweet Manufacturing Co., Ltd., P.O. Box 19, Ramat Gan, Israel

El Molino Mills, A.C.G. Company, City of Industry, California 91746

Estee Candy Company, Inc., 169 Lackawanna Avenue, Parsippany, New Jersey 07054

Fanny Farmer, Route 20 and Old State Road, Norwalk, Ohio 44587

Fanny Mae, 1137 West Jackson Boulevard, Chicago, Illinois 60607

Feodora (Zuckerrafinerie Tangermeunde Fr. Meyers Sohn), c/o Bahlsen of North America, Woodside, New York 11377

Ghirardelli Chocolate Company, 1111 139th Avenue, San Leandro, California 94578

Godiva Chocolatier, P.O. Box 5500, Norwalk, Connecticut 06856

Goya Foods, Inc. Meadow View Avenue, Secaucus, New Jersey

Halba, 8304 Wallisellen, Zurich, Switzerland

Hershey, Hershey Foods Corporation, Hershey, Pennsylvania 17033

Ibarra, c/o La Luz del Día, 624 North Main Street, Los Angeles, California 90012

Krön Chocolatier, 764 Madison Avenue, New York, New York 10021

Lenôtre Patissierie Traiteur, 42 Rue d'Auteuil, Paris 75106, France

Lindt & Sprungli A.G., 8802 Kilchberg, Zurich, Switzerland

The Maillard Corporation, 1300 Stefko Boulevard, Bethlehem, Pennsylvania 18018

Meshulam's, Inc. (Magic Nut Kitchens & Fruit Fair), 5978 Bowcroft Street, Los Angeles, California 90016

The Nestlé Company, 100 Bloomingdale Road, White Plains, New York 10605

Pangburn Company, Inc., P.O. Box 65, 1900 Southeast Loop 820, Fort Worth, Texas 76101

The Pennsylvania Dutch Company, Inc., P.O. Box 128, Manchester, Pennsylvania 17065

Pepperidge Farm, Confectionery Division, P.O. Box 5500, Norwalk, Connecticut 06956

Perugina U.S.A., 21 Main Street, Little Ferry, New Jersey (or I.B.P. Perugina, Via M. Angelonie 59, 06100 Perugia, Italy)

Russell Stover, 1004 Baltimore Avenue, Kansas City, Missouri 64105

See's Candies, 3423 South La Cienega Boulevard, Los Angeles, California 90016

Sprengel, c/o Richter Brothers, 355 Michelle Place, Carlstadt, New Jersey 07072 (or Sprengel, 3 Hannover, Gleunderstrasse 8, Germany)

Stuckey's Inc., P.O. Box 370, Eastman, Georgia 31023

Suchard American Corporation, 608 Fifth Avenue, New York, New York 10022

Joseph Terry & Sons, Ltd., Bishopthorpe Road, York Y01 1YE, England

Tobler Chocolat, 608 Fifth Avenue, New York, New York 10022

Van Houten & Zoon, Beemdelaan P.O. Box 120, Vaals, Holland

Whitman's Chocolate, 9701 Roosevelt Boulevard, Philadelphia, Pennsylvania 19105

Williams & Woods Ltd., 204 Parnell Street, Dublin, Ireland

World's Finest Chocolate, 2521 West 48 Street, Chicago, Illinois 60632

Zaanland, c/o Hermetica, Postbux 150, Zaandam, Holland

DIRECTORY OF CHOCOLATE TRADE ORGANIZATIONS

Chambre Syndicale National des Chocolatiers, 194 Rue de Rivoli, 75001 Paris, France

Chocolate Manufacturers of America, 7900 West Park Drive, McLean, Virginia 22101

Chocosuisse, Munzgraben 6, 3000 Bern 7, Switzerland

Cocoa, Chocolate and Confectionery Alliance, 11 Green Street, W1Y 3RF London, England

Conadeca, Tlaxcala 208, First Floor, Mexico 11 DF

INDEX

C

D

E

I

J

K

L

T

U

About the Author

Carol Ann Rinzler is a freelance writer who lives and works in New York.